© Copyright 2024 - All

The content contained within this book may not be duplicated or transmitted without direct written permission from the author or the publisher.

Under no circumstances will any blame or legal responsibility be held against the publisher, or author, for any damages, reparation, or monetary loss due to the information contained within this book, either directly or indirectly.

Legal Notice:

This book is copyright protected. It is only for personal use. You cannot amend, distribute, sell, use, quote or paraphrase any part, or the content within this book, without the consent of the author or publisher.

Disclaimer Notice:

Please note the information contained within this document is for educational and entertainment purposes only. All effort has been executed to present accurate, up to date, reliable, complete information. No warranties of any kind are declared or implied. Readers acknowledge that the author is not engaged in the rendering of legal, financial, medical or professional advice. The content within this book has been derived from various sources. Please consult a licensed professional before attempting any techniques outlined in this book.

By reading this document, the reader agrees that under no circumstances is the author responsible for any losses, direct or indirect, that are incurred as a result of the use of the information contained within this document, including, but not limited to, errors, omissions, or inaccuracies.

Calm in the Chaos

A Modern Guide to Managing Stress and Anxiety

Samson Greene

Table of Contents

INTRODUCTION 1

CHAPTER 1: UNDERSTANDING STRESS AND ANXIETY 5

   STRESS 6
      Stages of Stress 6
      What Causes Stress? 7
      What Are the Symptoms of Stress? 8
   ANXIETY 9
      What Causes Anxiety? 10
      What Are the Symptoms of Anxiety? 11
      Anxiety Disorders 13
   LONG-TERM EFFECTS OF STRESS AND ANXIETY 13
      Consequences of Chronic Stress and Anxiety 14
      The Ripple Effect 16
   CONCLUSION 17

CHAPTER 2: IDENTIFYING TRIGGERS AND PATTERNS 19

   COMMON TRIGGERS OF STRESS AND ANXIETY 20
      External Stressors 20
      Internal Stressors 21
      Anxiety Triggers 22
   SELF-MONITORING TECHNIQUES 23
      Daily Check-In 24
      Using the Mind-Body Connection 25
      Start a Stress Diary 26
   USING TECHNOLOGY TO TRACK STRESS MANAGEMENT 27
      Mobile Apps for Stress Tracking 28
      Wearable Devices 29
   CONCLUSION 30

CHAPTER 3: MINDFULNESS AND RELAXATION TECHNIQUES 33

   BASIC PRINCIPLES OF MINDFULNESS 34
      Mindful Awareness 35
      Breath Awareness 36
      Body Scan Technique 37

- PROGRESSIVE MUSCLE RELAXATION 38
  - *Benefits of Progressive Muscle Relaxation 38*
  - *How to Use This Technique 39*
- GROUNDING TECHNIQUES 41
  - *Sensory Grounding Techniques 41*
  - *Physical Grounding Techniques 42*
  - *Mental Grounding Techniques 42*
- CONCLUSION 43

CHAPTER 4: HEALTHY COPING STRATEGIES 45

- ENGAGING IN HOBBIES AND INTERESTS 46
  - *Benefits of Hobbies 47*
  - *Pursuing New Hobbies 47*
- STRESS RELIEF THROUGH CREATIVITY 48
  - *Art Therapy 49*
  - *Music 50*
- BALANCE BETWEEN WORK AND LEISURE 52
  - *Setting Boundaries 52*
  - *Planning Leisure Activities 53*
- CONCLUSION 54

CHAPTER 5: BUILDING EMOTIONAL RESILIENCE 57

- UNDERSTANDING EMOTIONAL INTELLIGENCE 58
  - *What Is Emotional Intelligence? 58*
  - *The Components of Emotional Intelligence 59*
  - *Emotional Intelligence in Managing Stress and Anxiety 60*
  - *How to Improve Your Emotional Intelligence 60*
- PRACTICING GRATITUDE 61
  - *Gratitude Journaling 62*
  - *Expressing Appreciation 64*
  - *Practicing Mindful Thankfulness 64*
- DEVELOPING A GROWTH MINDSET 65
  - *Embracing Challenges 66*
  - *Learning From Failures 66*
  - *Believing in Potential 67*
- CONCLUSION 67

CHAPTER 6: LIFESTYLE CHANGES FOR STRESS REDUCTION 69

- IMPORTANCE OF BALANCED NUTRITION 70
  - *Foods That Lower Stress and Anxiety 71*
  - *Foods to Avoid 72*
  - *Hydration 73*
- REGULAR PHYSICAL EXERCISE 73

 Sleep Hygiene 75
  Good Sleep Hygiene 76
 Avoiding Harmful Substances 77
  Nicotine 78
  Alcohol 79
 Conclusion 79

CHAPTER 7: CBT TECHNIQUES 81

 Challenging Negative Thoughts 82
  Types of Negative Thinking 82
  Cognitive Reframing 84
  Positive Affirmations 86
 Behavioral Activation 87
  Redirecting Your Thoughts 87
  Replacing Bad Habits 87
  Improving Your Relationships 88
 Conclusion 88

CHAPTER 8: SOCIAL SUPPORT AND COMMUNICATION SKILLS 91

 Benefits of Social Connections 92
  Types of Social Support 92
  Building a Support Network 94
  Importance of Social Support 94
 Effective Communication Techniques 95
  The 5 C's of Communication 96
  Active Listening 97
 Seeking Professional Help 98
  Support Groups 99
 Conclusion 100

CHAPTER 9: OVERCOMING FEAR AND WORRY 103

 Understanding the Nature of Fear 104
  Causes of Fear 104
  Effects of Fear 105
  Embracing Your Fears 106
 Exposure Therapy 107
  Benefits of Exposure Therapy 108
  Types of Exposure Therapy 108
 Conclusion 111

CONCLUSION 113

REFERENCES 117

Introduction

Do you ever feel like you are living life in a constant state of fight-or-flight? Like there is a sword hanging over your head, and everything will just come crashing down at any moment? It's sad how common it has become for us to exist in a perpetual state of panic. Stress and anxiety have become such a normal part of life for most of us. It's not surprising when you look at the fast-paced nature of modern society. Everything feels like an emergency, and people are always on the go. Between deadlines and appointments, it's hard to find time to breathe. I used to think this was normal, simply an expected byproduct of adulthood. I had bills and responsibilities, and people were counting on me. It did not faze me that I was always stressed, staring at my ceiling at 2 a.m., trying to figure out how I was going to meet my work quota and pay my bills on time.

I was one of those people who thought I worked well under pressure. The adrenaline of knowing I had a mountain of work to complete in a limited amount of time had so often given me the motivation I needed to get things done. I would laugh in relief—and a little disbelief—when I managed to finish a project on time. That momentary celebration was always short-lived because I was immediately onto the next one. The next urgent task, the next impossible deadline. I had no idea that I was running myself into the ground. I didn't even know what burnout was until it was too late. We forget that we have limits and that our bodies can only take so much. Eventually, something has to give.

It took me a long time to learn that there was another way to live and that I didn't need the threat of a deadline hanging over my head to perform at my best. It turns out I am actually a lot more productive when I am not overwhelmed with stress and anxiety. Believe it or not, being an adult is not about learning to work yourself to the bone or pushing yourself to the limits. It's not about losing hours of much-needed sleep obsessing over things you can't control or have no power to change. Anxiety does not need to be your constant companion. The process of learning how to overcome anxiety and effectively manage stress was a long and difficult journey. I bumped my head a few times along the way and wasted a lot of energy trying out some weird things I found on Reddit. Luckily for you, you will never need to fall asleep reading obscure medical journals.

This book is not about research and statistics. In this book, we will be exploring practical strategies that actually work. I won't bore you with lists of scientific data or regurgitating theoretical opinions. Sure, the things I am going to tell you are based on research, but I also understand that your stress and anxiety are not something you read about in a textbook. You are a real person, not just a statistic from a research paper. Your feelings and experiences are real, too, and that is why you need methods that are both practical and useful.

In this book, I am going to show you the things that worked for me when it came to learning how to manage and overcome my stress and anxiety. We'll be exploring the causes of these conditions and discussing the different ways they manifest. It is easier to deal with something when you understand what it is and where it comes from. Knowing the physical symptoms can also make it easier to spot them and become more aware of when they manifest in your life.

We'll also be delving into ways you can go about figuring out your triggers. This isn't so you can run away from these situations but so you can better prepare yourself to face them. Of course, you won't be going in blind. Using the tools and strategies we will discuss, you will be better equipped to deal with uncomfortable feelings when they arise. A life without stress or anxiety isn't possible. Anyone telling you they can eliminate them completely from your life is selling you a dream. But that doesn't mean that stress and anxiety need to control you!

What I am going to do is teach you how to manage your stress and cope with your anxiety. No longer will they hinder you from living a full life or limit your ability to function normally. When you learn how to live with your anxiety, you empower yourself to take back control of your life. You will no longer find yourself avoiding situations that could trigger it because you will know you have the tools to handle those situations without your anxiety getting the better of you.

Stress can cause a lot of problems and inevitably make the situation you are stressing about worse. When you learn how to manage your stress, you'll be better able to find solutions to your problems. Sometimes, stress can overwhelm and incapacitate you, leaving you unable to see a solution or feeling hopeless to overcome it. When you can remove the debilitating feeling that stress induces, you can think clearly.

The negative filter that stress colors your perspective can make things appear to be a lot worse than they are. By engaging with the useful techniques we will be exploring, you will find that your perspective shifts.

This book will be the beginning of your journey into a life no longer ruled by stress and dictated by anxiety. It's the first step to taking back your power and liberating yourself from the shackles that stress and anxiety have placed on you. By instilling you with practical tools and effective techniques to overcome their adverse effects, you can slowly begin to experience relief. You may not be able to undo the damage that stress and anxiety have caused you in the past, but you can certainly prevent them from negatively impacting you in the future.

This guide is about more than simply learning how to manage your stress and anxiety; it's about empowering you to face them head-on and giving you the confidence to know that they do not define you. My goal is to give you more than just helpful tips and practical strategies. I aim to provide you with something far more meaningful than that: *hope*.

Chapter 1:

Understanding Stress and Anxiety

The truth is that stress doesn't come from your boss, your kids, your spouse, traffic jams, health challenges, or other circumstances. It comes from your thoughts about your circumstances. –Andrew Bernstein

Before we begin, I'd like you to do three things: Stop frowning, unclench your jaw, and relax your shoulders. Feel better? You probably didn't even realize you were doing it. This is how our bodies react to stress and anxiety. It's so much more than what's going on in your mind; it extends to your body and manifests in many physical symptoms. This is just one example of how you are probably holding tension in your body constantly throughout the day. In this chapter, we will be exploring the physiological and psychological effects of stress and anxiety. In other words, how it affects your body and impacts your mind. Sometimes, releasing these tense emotions can be as simple as adjusting the way you are carrying them in your body. The exercise I suggested is just one of the many ways to start learning how to reprogram your mind using your body.

We will also be looking at some of the long-term effects of stress and anxiety. You might not think it's such a big deal right now. We are always so sure the stress will disappear as soon as we've found a solution to our problems, right? But does it? Probably not. Once you have trained yourself to exist in a constant state of stress, you will likely keep finding a reason to be stressed and anxious. It becomes a never-ending cycle. As soon as one situation is resolved, several others pop up in its place. The only way to keep that cycle from looping indefinitely is to break the habit. And, if you need a little extra nudge to get going, we'll look at how stress and anxiety will negatively impact you long-term. I'd like us to begin by learning more about stress and anxiety. What causes them, and what symptoms do they create? Once we have a better understanding of what we're dealing with, it will be simpler to formulate a plan to manage and overcome them.

Stress

Did you know that stress is not inherently negative? In the right amount, stress can actually be a very good thing. Stress is a biological reaction to a perceived threat; it is our primal instinct that lets us know we are in danger. Think back to the time of cavemen; a little stress could have meant the difference between life and death. Of course, stress has come to mean something different in our current context, but the same basic principles apply.

Stress is your body's way of letting you know that something urgent needs your attention. It triggers your fight-or-flight response and releases adrenaline and cortisol into your body, which will help you act accordingly. I am sure you have heard it said that too much of a good thing is a bad thing, and stress is no different. Too much stress can have dire implications for your physical and mental health.

Stages of Stress

Do you ever wonder what happens in your body when you are stressed? When you encounter a perceived threat or situation your mind perceives as dangerous, your body goes into fight-or-flight mode. In this phase, your brain releases chemicals into your blood that prepare you to face the stressor. The hormones of adrenaline and cortisol give you the energy you will need to either fight or run, and they also make your mind sharper and more focused. In this state, you are able to deal with the situation effectively. You might experience heart palpitations, notice that your breathing becomes shallow, and also have an increase in your blood pressure.

In a normal situation, these symptoms should be alleviated once the problem has been dealt with or the danger has passed. You should feel your body and senses slowly returning to normal. However, in the case of chronic stress, your mind and body kind of idle in that initial state of panic. This results in depleting your energy and mental reserves and can lead to burnout.

What Causes Stress?

The causes of stress are not universal. What might be stressful for one person might not necessarily be the case for someone else. For example, some people love socializing and attending lavish events. Others spend the whole year dreading the upcoming office Christmas party.

Stress can come about as the result of internal or external stressors. Let's look at some examples of both:

External Stressors

- work
- family
- money
- relationships
- health

The most significant cause of stress for most adults is work. Whether it be demanding work hours or an overwhelming workload, many people report experiencing chronic stress as a direct result of their careers. With the economy under strain, many people are really feeling the pinch. The stress of not knowing how you are going to pay the bills or not having the financial freedom to do the things you want can weigh you down.

Suffering from a chronic health condition or dealing with severe illness can also be extremely stressful. As fulfilling as it can feel to be in a healthy relationship, there's no doubt that romantic relationships take work. When conflict arises, it's normal to experience stress. However, some relationships become unhealthy when the level of stress they cause far outweighs the positive experiences.

Internal Stressors

- perfectionism
- low self-esteem
- negative self-talk
- unrealistic expectations
- pessimism

Internal stressors are things that come from inside yourself. They can be triggered by external events that negatively affect how you think about and see yourself. They can also stem from feelings of worthlessness, hopelessness, unlovability, or failure.

Many of your internal stressors might stem from the way you view yourself and the world, especially when reality doesn't match your expectations. The best way to combat these thoughts and feelings is to change your perception, but we'll get into that later.

What Are the Symptoms of Stress?

As much as different people have different triggers of stress, it also manifests in various ways. However, there are a few common symptoms that might indicate you are under a lot of stress. These include:

- fatigue
- insomnia
- changes in appetite
- changes in libido

- acne
- headaches
- irritability
- gastrointestinal problems (nausea, diarrhea, stomach pain)
- vertigo
- heart palpitations, hyperventilating

You may experience any number of these symptoms when you are under stress, but you are not likely to experience all of them. I used to know I was extremely stressed when my skin broke out. It was always my telltale sign that it was time to sit down and reevaluate some things! Maybe you have a specific symptom that alerts you to the fact that you are taking on too much. Never ignore these signs; they are your body's way of warning you that it is under strain. Think of these symptoms as your early warning signal that it's time to do something about the situation before things get worse.

Anxiety

Anxiety is that feeling of discomfort, nervousness, and unease you get in the pit of your stomach. Unlike fear, which comes about as the result of an imminent threat or immediate danger, anxiety doesn't necessarily have an urgent underlying stressor. It is more of a reaction to a perceived threat, whether real or imagined.

Much like with stress, a healthy amount of anxiety can be a good thing. It can give you the push you need to get things done or motivate you to reach your goals. However, in unhealthy amounts, anxiety can be incapacitating. In extreme amounts, it can become a medical condition that severely impacts your quality of life.

Imagine being terrified of everyone and everything all of the time. That is what anxiety feels like. It is like starring in a real-life adaptation of a horror movie where all your worst fears and phobias are lurking around every corner. People who suffer from anxiety find it difficult to live a normal life because even the most basic tasks can trigger such feelings of terror that they can't function optimally. In some cases, anxiety can prevent you from achieving your goals because the fear of failure stops you from even trying.

I used to work at a job where I was passed up for a promotion for several years in a row. Each year, I sat silently seething because my juniors were being elevated above me in a company I'd dedicated so much of my life to. And even though I was qualified and had put in the work, my anxiety had always prevented me from applying for a promotion. Instead, I sat in silence, being resentful. When I finally overcame that anxiety just long enough to fill in the paperwork, I was surprised to realize that they'd been more than willing to promote me for years if only I had applied. I knew then that my anxiety had been stifling my growth, and I wondered how many other opportunities had passed me by because of this. You might not even be aware of the ways your anxiety has been holding you back until you finally overcome it. Anxiety that motivates you to do something is healthy, but when your anxiety prevents you from acting, it's a problem.

What Causes Anxiety?

Anxiety is often caused by a fear of the future and uncertainty. It can occur in anticipation of something that might happen or even by nothing at all. Normally, this feeling should subside once you have allowed yourself the time to work through the fear. But for some people, that fear overwhelms their ability to think critically and solve problems. In these cases, anxiety becomes a hindrance to a person's ability to function normally. Although anxiety does not have one known cause, several factors influence your susceptibility to experiencing high levels of anxiety.

Some of these include:

- a family history of anxiety
- learned coping mechanisms
- chronic stress
- traumatic events
- certain substances and medications
- medical conditions

There are some other risk factors that influence the likelihood of you suffering from anxiety, such as your age, ethnicity, environment, and upbringing. What matters isn't what has caused your anxiety or where it comes from but what you can do to manage and overcome it.

What Are the Symptoms of Anxiety?

Anxiety can be a pretty uncomfortable feeling to live with. It skews your perception of reality and turns everything and everyone around you into a threat. It is like your fight-or-flight mechanisms are working in overdrive.

Psychological Signs

Some of the psychological signs you can look out for that might indicate suffering from anxiety are:

- paranoia
- restlessness
- insomnia
- irritability

- irrational fears and phobias

- difficulty concentrating

- agitation

If you often find yourself feeling on edge and constantly looking over your shoulder, you might be suffering from anxiety. Again, a healthy level of anxiety can be helpful. For example, when you are walking home alone at night, anxiety will make sure you stay vigilant of your surroundings.

However, if you are at a child's birthday party, jumping at every loud sound and looking around every corner, your anxiety might be getting the better of you.

Physical Symptoms

Much like stress, anxiety also affects your body. It can be experienced in many ways, and every person is unique. These are the most common physical symptoms of anxiety:

- sweating

- shortness of breath

- trembling

- headache

- heart palpitations

- nausea

Many people experience these symptoms at some point during their day, but not consistently in a never-ending loop. Having your mind and body on high alert all the time is unhealthy and will eventually lead to more serious health complications.

Anxiety Disorders

When anxiety reaches its most extreme form, it can result in a mental disorder. Anxiety disorders are the leading mental condition in America, affecting a large portion of the population. There are many different types of anxiety disorders, each affecting people differently and to varying degrees.

Some of the most common anxiety disorders are:

- generalized anxiety disorder
- social anxiety disorder (or social phobia)
- panic disorder
- phobias
- separation anxiety disorder
- selective mutism

Anxiety disorders may begin in childhood and slowly become more severe as you get older. By the time you reach adulthood, an anxiety disorder might reach a point where you are no longer able to perform daily tasks or live a normal life. In the case of an anxiety disorder, it is advised that you seek professional medical treatment. As much as you can help curb some of the more debilitating effects of your disorder through self-help techniques, in these cases, medical intervention is the most effective treatment option.

Long-Term Effects of Stress and Anxiety

I've mentioned several times that stress and anxiety can have a severe impact on your health in the long run. Now, we're going to explore this a little further. You are probably wondering how a natural mechanism can cause long-term damage. Well, when stress and anxiety become chronic, they take up a lot more energy than they're supposed to, and your body ends up secreting a lot more adrenaline and cortisol than it usually would.

When we look at the physical symptoms of stress or anxiety, such as heart palpitations, shortness of breath, and muscle tension, we can get a glimpse into the possible complications. These three bodily reactions work those organs harder than they would under normal circumstances. Now, imagine that heightened mechanism working in overdrive over an extended period of time. Doesn't sound too good, right?

Let's break it down even further by exploring each of these mechanisms individually and looking at how stress and anxiety negatively impact them over time:

Consequences of Chronic Stress and Anxiety

Cardiovascular Health

Stress and anxiety cause your heart rate to increase and may cause heart palpitations or chest pains. When this happens constantly, your heart takes strain. As a result, this increases your risk of:

- heart attack
- stroke
- high blood pressure
- heart disease

Digestive Health

When you are stressed, your liver produces excess glucose to give you an added energy boost. When you are constantly stressed, your body ends up having more glucose in the blood than it knows what to do with. This can lead to type 2 diabetes. Stress also interrupts the way your body digests food, and as such, you may experience gastrointestinal disturbances such as diarrhea, constipation, nausea, and vomiting.

Stress does not cause ulcers, but it can exacerbate existing ones. The increase in stomach acid caused by stress can also lead to heartburn and acid reflux.

Muscular Health

Your body reacts to stress by tensing up your muscles, preparing you to either fight or run. In a normal situation, your muscles should relax once the stress wears off. However, when you are constantly stressed, they never get the opportunity to. This can lead to chronic muscle pain, backache, and headaches.

Central Nervous System Health

The hormones released when you are stressed can wreak havoc on your brain. Long-term exposure to cortisol can affect your memory and cause dizziness, headaches, and depression. The high level of cortisol could also contribute to weight gain.

Sexual Health

As you can imagine, stress can cause you to lose your libido. However, the impact doesn't just stop there. In men, chronic stress can lead to erectile dysfunction and negatively affect their sperm production, making it harder to conceive.

For women, it also lowers fertility by interrupting their menstrual cycle. In some cases, women can stop menstruating altogether as a result of chronic stress.

Immune System Health

Continuous exposure to stress can lower your immune system's ability to fight off infection. It also decreases your body's ability to respond to foreign invaders, increasing your risk of developing cancer. Chronic stress additionally causes your body to take much longer to recover from illnesses.

Mental Health

As you can see, chronic stress has far-reaching health implications, impacting every aspect of your body's organs and their ability to function. However, the health effects of stress don't stop at a psychological level. They can also influence your mental health.

Stress has been known to alter your nervous system, specifically impacting the parts of your brain responsible for memory, problem-solving, and attentiveness. As a result, people who suffer from chronic stress often find it difficult to concentrate for long periods, experience lapses in their memory, and struggle to learn new things or retain new information.

Chronic stress and anxiety can also change your personality, and you will find yourself exhibiting traits and experiencing things you never had before. Things like being extremely short-tempered and irritable, losing interest in things you love, and isolating yourself from your loved ones are all common symptoms of chronic stress and anxiety. You might also find yourself not caring about your appearance or the upkeep of your hygiene or acting impulsively.

The Ripple Effect

The effects of chronic stress and anxiety aren't just limited to you either. They also impact other areas of your life and your relationships with the people around you. It can ripple out to your work, relationships, and social life.

Relationship Strain

Chronic stress can strain relationships by affecting communication, empathy, and patience. When stressed, we may become irritable or withdraw emotionally, impacting our interactions with loved ones.

Decreased Work Productivity

Stress can impair cognitive function, focus, and decision-making. As a result, productivity at work or in daily tasks may decline. It's essential to manage stress to maintain optimal performance.

Social Withdrawal

High stress levels often lead to social withdrawal. We might avoid social gatherings, isolate ourselves, or feel overwhelmed by social interactions. Connecting with others is crucial for our well-being, so managing stress is vital.

Conclusion

I know you probably feel like you just sat through an episode of "Scared Straight," but my intention is not to frighten you. By looking closely at what stress and anxiety are, what causes them, and how they are impacting your health and life, I am hoping to put them into perspective. Once you realize the serious health implications of chronic stress and anxiety, you will become aware that stress shouldn't just be a regular part of your life and that anxiety isn't an ideal coping mechanism.

By learning more about stress and anxiety and seeing the long-term consequences, I'm hoping you will be able to motivate yourself to nip them in the bud. It turns out your constant worrying will cause you more than a few extra wrinkles on your forehead as you get older.

Instead, it's going to put you at risk of a whole host of medical conditions that you could avoid by learning how to get your stress and anxiety under control. I hope this chapter has opened your eyes to what you are dealing with and given you a fresh perspective on the things you have been sweeping under the rug. So, now that we know what we're dealing with, let's start looking at ways to curb those unhealthy habits.

Chapter 2:

Identifying Triggers and Patterns

Avoiding your triggers isn't healing. Healing happens when you're triggered, and you're able to move through the pain, the pattern, and the story and walk your way to a different ending. –Vienna Pharaon

I used to get so anxious around Christmas and family gatherings, and for so long, I had no idea why. I could feel myself start to stress in anticipation weeks before, already dreading the prospect. I would sit up at night trying to figure out a way to keep working right through them, as if by drowning myself in work, I could avoid whatever I was feeling altogether. That was always how I'd done things, hiding behind my deadlines and career aspirations so I wouldn't have to face life. And it worked for a while. I guess the more I excelled at work, the less I had to admit that I hadn't progressed in other aspects of my life.

It took me many years to finally understand that the anxiety I experienced around those times wasn't necessarily centered around the events themselves but around the celebrations with my family. The more I honed in on the feeling, the more I became aware that family events made me uncomfortable. I mean, don't we all get stressed when it comes to those awkward get-togethers? I'm cringing just thinking about it. I always knew that people were going to ask me inappropriately personal questions I didn't want to answer.

Realizing the trigger of my stress and anxiety was such a relief. I could finally distill the feeling into something that made sense instead of a general assumption that I didn't enjoy the holidays. Of course, I couldn't just decide to never attend family occasions again. Going cold turkey at Christmas with the family simply wasn't an option, pun intended. However, identifying the trigger was an essential first step. I wouldn't ever have been able to find ways to deal with those feelings otherwise.

In this chapter, I'll teach you how to identify the people and situations that might be triggering your stress and anxiety. By gaining an awareness of where the feelings are coming from, you will empower yourself to better solve them.

Common Triggers of Stress and Anxiety

A trigger can be any situation that produces feelings of stress and anxiety. Of course, these vary from person to person. An experience that might cause you to feel anxious might not have the same effect on another person. Being able to identify your triggers can make managing your stress so much easier because it removes the feeling of fighting an invisible enemy.

Stressors come in many different forms, but we can separate them into two distinct categories: external and internal. Differentiating between these stressors is important because they need to be handled in different ways. An external stressor happens to you, whereas an internal stressor is something you create. Knowing how to deal with each of these will give you the ability to control how they impact you in daily life. Let's take a closer look at each of these.

External Stressors

An external stressor is a trigger that occurs as a result of something happening in the world around you. It can often be attributed to something that's out of your control. External stressors can be anything from a major natural disaster to getting stuck in a traffic jam on your way home.

Since external stressors are out of your control, the best way to deal with them is to change how you react to them. You can't choose what happens to you, but you can decide how you let it affect you.

Some examples of external stressors could be:

- work (things like deadlines, having too much work to do, or working long hours)

- relationships (having conflicts with friends or family members)

- financial (an unexpected expense such as your car breaking down, your rent going up, inflation, or a recession)

- health (suddenly falling ill, having a medical condition that impedes your ability to function normally, or sustaining an injury that impairs you temporarily)

- traumatic events (losing a loved one or a death, natural disaster, being a victim of a violent crime)

- major life changes (losing a job, having to move suddenly, divorce, marriage, buying a house)

Any event, experience, or environment that impacts your daily life can cause stress, whether it is positive or negative. Since we can't control what happens to us, the best way to handle these situations is to change our attitude toward them. In essence, before you can learn to cope with external stressors, you should first master how to handle your internal stressors.

Internal Stressors

Internal stressors are caused by ourselves. They can result from your beliefs, perceptions, and how you see yourself. When you view the world a certain way, and reality doesn't live up to your expectations, this can cause stress.

Your thoughts and emotions can also cause you internal stress, especially if you are overly critical of yourself or judge yourself too harshly.

Some good examples of internal stressors are:

- low self-esteem
- negative self-talk
- perfectionism
- unrealistic expectations for yourself
- pessimistic attitude

When you constantly have a negative dialogue going on in your head, it's no surprise that you might find yourself constantly under stress. The best way to combat these kinds of internal stressors is to change your way of thinking. I know this is easier said than done, but that doesn't mean it's impossible. Once you have gotten a handle on a good technique for dealing with your internal stressors, you will find it much easier to apply those same principles to managing your external stressors, too.

Anxiety Triggers

Although each person has a unique set of triggers, there are certain situations that are commonly found to be triggering for people who suffer from anxiety.

A few of them are:

- health issues or receiving a difficult diagnosis
- parties and events or large gatherings of people
- certain medications
- caffeine
- an unhealthy diet or skipping meals

- public events or performances and public speaking

- negative thinking

- anything that reminds you of a negative experience you might have had in the past

As I've said before, knowing your triggers isn't about avoiding them or isolating yourself so you never have to face them. Finding out what your triggers are is the first step toward empowering yourself to overcome them. When you know you are about to face a situation that can trigger your anxiety, you can give yourself the opportunity to prepare for it. You will find this makes it so much easier than just being blindsided by it.

Self-Monitoring Techniques

If, like me, you sat for hours in front of an empty page and couldn't identify a single trigger, that is okay! You are not alone in your confusion. I was shocked when I realized that, despite how much stress and anxiety I experienced daily, I couldn't isolate a single incident or trace a pattern that could give me clues.

A lot of the time, we're not consciously aware of when the triggers are happening because we're so consumed by the uncomfortable feelings we're experiencing and desperately trying to figure out how we can get away from the situation. And then, once we're out of the situation, we're not inclined to sit and reflect on it. We don't really want to dissect it to figure out what caused it and how we can handle it better in the future. Most of us just want to sweep it under the rug and move on. Unfortunately, that's not the best idea. Without keeping track of these triggering events, we'll never make any progress in learning how to cope with these feelings.

When you become more aware of the situations and scenarios that trigger your anxiety and start keeping track of the incidents, you can give yourself the gift of clarity. Each isolated incident might feel haphazard, but once you begin to see them all laid out, you might start seeing a pattern emerge. This is how you will begin to identify your triggers. Let's look at three easy tools you can use to start becoming more aware of your stress and anxiety and help you on your way to identifying your triggers:

Daily Check-In

We often get so caught up in life that we forget to take some time to do a wellness check on ourselves. Setting aside some time each day to check in with yourself is a significant first step to becoming more aware of your triggers.

Take a few moments at the end of your day to reflect on any situations that may have caused you stress and anxiety. It might also be helpful to write these down so you can keep a record of them.

Ask yourself questions like:

- Why did I feel anxious/stressed today?
- Have I felt this way in this situation before?
- What about this person/situation triggered these feelings?
- How did I handle the situation?
- How can I handle it better in the future?

When you pause to reflect on your day like this, you might find that you gain a different perspective on what's happened. In the heat of the moment, we sometimes don't make the best decision. We act on impulse and react based on our emotions. You might find more clarity in the comfort of your home, away from the triggering situations. You might even realize that you are proud of the way you handled yourself and can give yourself a pat on the back! Don't beat yourself up if you feel you might have overreacted or behaved inappropriately. Mistakes are how we learn.

By reflecting back on the situation, you can come up with better ways to respond if you ever find yourself in that position again. No matter the outcome, being able to reflect on these situations and assess them will give you a better understanding not only of yourself and how your stress and anxiety are affecting you, but it might also help illuminate a common thread between the scenarios where you find yourself experiencing these feelings. You will be able to identify your triggers *and* come up with practical ways to handle them in the future.

Using the Mind-Body Connection

We've spoken about how stress and anxiety affect you not just mentally but also physiologically. Sometimes, it's easier to be aware of the symptoms than the underlying emotions. Another way you can go about identifying your triggers is by tracking the physical symptoms you experience as a result of stress and anxiety and then linking them to the events leading up to them. Here are some practical ways for you to track the physical symptoms related to stress and anxiety:

Symptom Journal

Keep a symptom journal to record any physical symptoms you experience throughout the day. Make sure you take note of:

- the date
- time
- details of the symptom (e.g., headache, stomachache, heart palpitations, sweating).

Trigger Analysis

Whenever you notice a symptom, take a moment to reflect on what might have triggered it. Was it a work deadline, an argument, or a specific situation? Write down your thoughts and observations.

Patterns and Associations

Over time, look for patterns. Do certain stressors consistently lead to specific symptoms? For example:

- Do you always get headaches after intense work meetings?
- Are you constantly getting stomachaches during family gatherings?
- Have you always gotten muscle tension in large gatherings?

When you become more keenly aware of when you are experiencing symptoms, you make it so much simpler to figure out what events might be causing them. Now, I'm not saying that you can blame your mother-in-law for your ulcer, but you will be better able to see the correlation between specific situations and how your stress symptoms manifest. By keeping track of your symptoms, you can learn so much more about not just your triggers but the different ways that your body reacts to your stress and anxiety. This will also make learning how to manage and overcome them that much easier.

Start a Stress Diary

I know we often associate writing in a journal with the image of a teenage girl wielding a glitter pen, but you'd be surprised by how effective daily journaling can be in tracking and managing your stress. When you keep a daily journal where you record your experiences, you can get a clearer picture of how your stress and anxiety are affecting you daily.

You also gain self-awareness when you can look back on past entries and see how you might be repeating the same negative reactions in similar situations. It's also a great way to track your progress when you can look back and see how much you've improved over time.

Try to schedule a few minutes at the end of your day where you can write in your stress diary. Include the following:

- Were there any situations where you felt stressed or anxious? What might have been the cause?

- How did you feel in these situations? What emotions came up for you?

- Are there any physical symptoms you may have experienced that were caused by stress and anxiety?

- Point out any triggers that consistently affect you and how you might handle them better in the future.

- Rate your stress and anxiety for that day on a scale of 1–10

Keeping a stress diary isn't just about learning more about your triggers; it's also about learning more about yourself. Sometimes, it's easier to make sense of your thoughts when you get them outside of your head. Seeing things written down can help you realize that you might have made a mountain out of a molehill and maybe even give you the opportunity to laugh at yourself if you've been a tad dramatic. The greatest benefit of tracking your progress is being able to look back and see all the improvements you've made. Often, it's difficult to see much of a change from one day to the next, but when you're able to look back weeks or even months, you can gain a better appreciation of your efforts.

Using Technology to Track Stress Management

Living in the digital age, it's not surprising that there's an app for everything. Since we're always on our phones, why not use them to help us learn how to manage our stress and anxiety? There have been so many amazing advancements in technology that enable us to do just that. Stress tracking is so much more than just ticking off a list of your symptoms and waiting for a robot to regurgitate a bunch of facts for you. These days, you can even get wearable devices that track your heart rate and send you an alert when you are experiencing elevated levels of stress.

Using a stress tracker is an added bonus for those of us who are constantly on the go and might forget to pause and log an event in our stress journal. It can even be that gentle hand on your shoulder telling you to calm down and take a deep breath when you are seconds away from blowing your top.

Let's take a look at some of the most effective ways to use technology to help you on your stress management journey.

Mobile Apps for Stress Tracking

Several apps are available for download online that can be very helpful in learning how to identify and manage your triggers, track your stress and anxiety, and offer practical strategies and coping mechanisms. Depending on your needs and goals, you can choose between a variety of platforms that offer tailored help for managing daily stress and anxiety.

Some of the features available on stress tracking apps are:

- mood tracking
- daily reminders
- insights into your mood patterns
- forums available for emotional support
- practical strategies for managing your stress and anxiety
- tracking your lifestyle and eating habits
- goals and activity tracking

It's so much easier for some of us to quickly log a few symptoms and feelings than to sit down and write in a journal. It also takes less time, and the insights offered might give you a different perspective than if you were just looking back on your thoughts. The forums might also give you an extra sense of understanding by reading about people who are dealing with the same struggles as you are and getting feedback from them on what has worked in their own experiences.

Wearable Devices

There are a few devices that can help you manage stress by tracking things like your heart rate, skin temperature, and breathing. These wearable devices can come in the form of a watch, a headband, or something you can clip to your waistband.

By using a wearable device to track your stress, you can get a more comprehensive idea of how your stress affects you throughout the day. Since the app tracks your stress levels in real time, you can look back and see the increases and decreases in your stress for that day and calculate what might have been happening at that time. You can also spot trends by evaluating data collected over an extended period.

Another benefit of wearable devices is that they work alongside other health-tracking apps. This will allow you to weigh your stress levels against things like your fitness levels, sleeping schedule, and other metrics collected by your health apps. You will then be able to paint a much clearer picture of which aspects of your life are negatively impacting your stress levels and what strategies would work best to combat this.

Some wearable devices offer an added bonus: In addition to tracking your stress, they also help you counteract its effects. For example, some devices deliver vibrating pulses to help calm you down if you are exhibiting signs of stress, and others send you meditative exercises to soothe your anxiety.

The industry of stress-tracking wearable devices is still fairly new and constantly expanding. Companies are continuously releasing new updates that offer users more features to help track and manage their stress. It might be a little costly to buy the devices, and some apps require a monthly subscription fee, but it's certainly an investment worth considering.

Conclusion

Identifying your triggers is an essential component of learning how to better manage your stress. By simply becoming aware of the specifics behind what situations and experiences are causing you to become anxious or stressed, you have already taken a huge leap in your journey to freedom. Although, as we've learned, self-awareness is only a part of the solution. Knowing your triggers can take the sting out of that feeling of being caught off guard, but you risk falling into the trap of avoidance.

I know it can be tempting to avoid places and scenarios that might trigger you, but this isn't a long-term solution. Instead, you will end up isolating yourself and hiding from the world. When you hide from your stress and anxiety, you are letting them get the better of you. Instead, you can empower yourself to face these situations head-on by learning ways to manage your stress.

Incorporating stress-tracking exercises into your daily routine is a great way to start learning more about how stress and anxiety manifest in your life. By allowing yourself a few minutes at the end of your day to practice daily check-ins, write in a stress diary, or even use your physical symptoms to identify triggers, you can start understanding yourself more. You can assess situations and come up with ways to better handle yourself in the future. Of course, not everybody has the time to do that, and some of us can be extremely forgetful. Thanks to advancements in technology, this doesn't need to stop you.

Stress-tracking apps and wearable devices can give you an edge when it comes to gaining insights into your stress levels throughout the day. By using these apps in conjunction with other health monitoring apps, you can get a more holistic view of how your stress affects your life and what measures you can take to manage it better.

Now that you have got a handle on your triggers and have gleaned some insights into the patterns behind your stress and anxiety, you are in a better position to start formulating a tangible action plan on how you are going to overcome them.

Chapter 3:

Mindfulness and Relaxation Techniques

Mindfulness is cultivated by assuming the stance of an impartial witness to your own experience. To do this requires that you become aware of the constant stream of judging and reacting to inner and outer experiences that we are all normally caught up in and learn to step back from it. –Kabat Zinn

I had always associated meditation with people who named themselves after plants and didn't wear shoes. That was the mental image I got any time someone tried to tell me about how mindfulness was changing their lives and improving their mental health. I figured it was only a matter of time before they turned vegan and stopped wearing shoes. As a result of my judgments and slight ignorance, I spent years missing out on the incredible benefits of adopting mindfulness strategies. When it comes to managing stress and anxiety, mindfulness is like the holy grail. As someone whose mind was constantly fixated on the future and all the uncertainty it held, learning how to stay firmly rooted in the present has been one of the most powerful tools in my arsenal when it comes to dealing with people and situations that trigger my anxiety and cause me stress.

In this chapter, we'll be delving into the practice of mindfulness. Not in the way you have probably assumed it to be, but in a practical way that can give you tools you can turn to for daily relief from your stress and anxiety. By incorporating mindfulness and some relaxation techniques into your daily routine, you can help yourself to stay grounded. It can serve as a constant reminder to stay grounded in the present moment and can also offer you a way to combat the effects of stress and anxiety in real time.

Basic Principles of Mindfulness

Before we explore the benefits of mindfulness in managing stress and anxiety, let's first look at what it is. Mindfulness, in essence, is the practice of being fully present in the moment. It allows you to immerse yourself in your current experiences, observe your thoughts without judgment, and understand your emotions without being controlled by them. When you practice mindfulness, you are able to make better decisions, see situations clearer, and gain a deeper understanding of yourself and the world around you.

The benefits of mindfulness have been well-documented and backed up by research, which definitely cured me of my trepidation. Yes, it has its roots in Eastern philosophy and Buddhism, but over the last few decades, it has been adopted by Western culture and formed the basis of new ways of treating mental health. You see, when you are stressed or anxious, a lot of those feelings stem from the fact that your mind is constantly thinking about the future. You are analyzing the outcomes of events that have yet to transpire, in some cases, events that probably never will. When you become more mindful, you are faced only with the here and now. Your mind is focused on your current experience, helping relieve you of those thoughts.

Some of the ways practicing mindfulness can help alleviate stress and anxiety include:

- By accepting your feelings, you won't be overwhelmed by them.

- Focusing on the present moment prevents you from being distracted by fears for the future.

- Observing your emotions without judgment helps keep negative self-talk and other pessimistic attitudes from impacting your perception of reality.

- Being aware of the sensations in your body can help you cope with the physical symptoms of stress and anxiety.

Mindful Awareness

Now that you know what mindfulness is and why you need it, you are probably wondering how to start implementing it in your life. I'm so glad that you asked! Mindfulness can be a little tricky at first, especially when you have become so accustomed to your mind racing at a hundred miles per hour, so it's best to start small and take it slow. You are not going to become an expert overnight, so don't expect that you will be able to sit in silent meditation for two hours on the first day.

Mindfulness is more than just meditation, although that is a part of it. A good place to start would be by practicing mindful awareness. Training your mind to become more aware and present takes time and patience. Practicing mindful awareness is the first step. Being mindfully aware means taking note of what is happening both around you and inside you as it happens.

This means connecting with your senses to acknowledge what's happening in the world around you. It also means observing your thoughts and emotions as if you were merely a spectator, without judgment.

Let's take a real-life example. Your boss has just asked you to come to his office at lunch. Immediately, your mind begins conjuring up a million possibilities of what this might mean. You probably spiral from thinking your work isn't up to par and end up convinced you are either facing disciplinary action or about to lose your job. Practicing mindful awareness in this situation means pulling your thoughts away from the future and into the present.

You can start by reminding yourself that it's only 10 a.m., and lunch isn't for another three hours. Instead of spending that time stressing about what might happen and anxious about how you are going to react, take each moment as it comes. Focus on what you are doing, and accept that whatever will happen will happen, whether you stress about it or not. Pay attention to the sensations of stress and anxiety you are experiencing in your body. Notice if your palms are sweaty, your heart is racing, or your muscles are tensing. Then, become aware of your emotions—but by simply observing them.

When you separate your present experience from your perceived reality, you can gain better control. Emotions tend to cloud your judgment and make it harder to make rational decisions; mindful awareness alleviates this by giving you the power to accept them.

By practicing mindful awareness throughout your day, you will find that the impact of stress and anxiety over your experiences is lessened. It's not that you won't experience them, but they won't dictate your thoughts and emotions like they once did. You can pause, acknowledge them, process them, and move on. Right now, I know that's easier said than done, but over time, this will become a habit and much easier.

Breath Awareness

Have you ever been told to take a few deep breaths to calm down? Then, you have been practicing mindfulness without knowing! Breath awareness is a very useful technique for mindfulness because it forces you to become fully present in your body. Breath awareness, or conscious breathing, is the act of observing your breathing without altering it. You draw your attention to the flow of breath in and out of your lungs. It sounds simple, but it can have a profound effect on your overall mental and emotional well-being.

The great thing about this mindfulness technique is that you can do it anytime, anywhere, and as often as you need. When you are feeling overwhelmed by a situation, simply take a moment to breathe, even if that means excusing yourself from the room and sitting outside for a few minutes. Close your eyes and focus on nothing but your breathing. If your mind starts to wander to the situation that triggered you, gently draw it back to your breathing. As you breathe, you will slowly feel your body begin to relax and your thoughts become calmer. Now, you are in a better frame of mind to face whatever might have triggered you.

There are many other breathing techniques you might want to explore along the way, but this is the most basic. As you find your feet and get more comfortable with it, you can look up different methods online or by downloading a meditation app.

Body Scan Technique

The body scan meditation is a mindfulness technique where you systematically draw your attention to different parts of your body. During the body scan, you become aware of the sensations going through each part of your body, noticing any areas where you might be holding stress and tension and allowing yourself to release it.

The body scan meditation can be incredibly useful when you are experiencing an overwhelming amount of stress and anxiety. Not only does it allow you to become more aware of where you are experiencing the physical symptoms, but it also distracts your mind from dwelling on whatever might be causing it. It will leave you feeling more relaxed in your body and calmer in your mind.

Here's how you can practice the body scan technique:

1. Find a comfortable position for yourself, either seated or lying down.
2. Close your eyes to prevent distractions.
3. Focus on your breath, keeping it steady and even.
4. Starting at the top of your head, begin becoming aware of the sensations you are experiencing.
5. Focus on this area for at least 30 seconds before moving on.
6. If you feel your mind beginning to drift, gently pull yourself back to the present moment.

7. Work your way down your body slowly, giving each part of yourself enough time to fully become aware of the sensations you are experiencing.

8. At the end, take several moments to refocus on your breathing before ending the meditation.

Like with any other tool or strategy, you will need to practice this technique often because you will notice the positive effects through consistently using it. When you get into the habit of regularly connecting with your body, you will find that you become so much more in tune with the symptoms of your stress and anxiety, and it becomes easier over time to release the tension and alleviate the discomfort.

Progressive Muscle Relaxation

Remember when I asked you to unclench your jaw and relax your shoulders? Did it surprise you to realize that you were doing it? You are definitely not alone! Many people aren't aware enough of their bodies to understand when they're experiencing tension in their muscles. Progressive muscle relaxation, or PMR, is one of the best techniques you can use to combat this.

PMR is a technique used to induce relaxation by tensing and releasing the muscles of your body in a particular order or pattern. By first tensing and then releasing these muscles, you can become more aware of what it feels like when you are not in a relaxed state. As you get into the habit of regularly practicing PMR, it will become easier for you to immediately notice when you are experiencing tension in any part of your body.

Benefits of Progressive Muscle Relaxation

Some of the many benefits you can gain from practicing PMR are:

- relief from the symptoms of anxiety

- reduced tension

- improved sleep

- reduced pain in your lower back and neck

- improved blood pressure

- reduced occurrence of migraines

How to Use This Technique

Before we get into the how, I want to add that this technique should not be used if you have an injury or suffer from muscle spasms, as it could worsen your condition.

Here is a step-by-step guide on how to practice PMR:

1. Start by sitting or lying down; make sure you are feeling completely relaxed.

2. Take a few deep, slow breaths, allowing yourself to further sink into your relaxation.

3. Lift your toes upward. Tense and hold for a few seconds, and then release.

4. Point your toes downward. Tense and hold for a few seconds, and then release.

5. Pull your knees up toward your body. Tense and hold for a few seconds, and then release.

6. Squeeze the muscles in your thighs. Tense and hold for a few seconds, and then release.

7. Clench your hands into fists. Tense and hold for a few seconds, and then release.

8. Tighten up the muscles in your arms. Tense and hold for a few seconds, and then release.

9. Clench your butt cheeks together. Tense and hold for a few seconds, and then release.

10. Squeeze the muscles in your abdomen. Tense and hold for a few seconds, and then release.

11. Take a deep breath to tighten the muscles in your chest. Tense and hold for a few seconds, and then release.

12. Lift your shoulders up to your ears. Tense and hold for a few seconds, and then release.

13. Press your lips together hard. Tense and hold for a few seconds, and then release.

14. Open your mouth as wide as you can. Tense and hold for a few seconds, and then release.

15. Squeeze your eyes shut. Tense and hold for a few seconds, and then release.

16. Raise your eyebrows. Tense and hold for a few seconds, and then release.

Through regular practice of this technique, you will become a lot more aware of these small, sometimes unnoticeable contractions in your muscles that often lead to chronic pain. You will notice that some of these sensations feel overly familiar when you tense the muscles in those areas.

These are the many ways our bodies react to stress, and you have probably been tensing up those muscles so often and for so long that you have forgotten what they feel like in their relaxed state. Sometimes, while doing this exercise, I find myself about to tense a muscle only to realize that it's already clenched by default!

Making this technique a regular habit will not only alleviate the pain but also help you feel a lot more relaxed overall and improve the physical symptoms associated with your stress and anxiety.

Grounding Techniques

Grounding is a useful tool when you are feeling overwhelmed by your thoughts and emotions. By grounding you in the present moment, it helps alleviate the symptoms of stress and anxiety by distracting you from your immediate environment.

Grounding techniques have proven extremely effective in managing stress and anxiety and can lead to better sleep and emotional regulation. There are three main types of grounding techniques. Let's explore each of them more in-depth.

Sensory Grounding Techniques

Sensory grounding techniques employ your five senses to attune you to things you normally wouldn't really notice in your immediate environment. By fully engaging your mind and senses, you give yourself a way to diffuse overwhelming thoughts and feelings.

The 5-4-3-2-1 Method

An excellent method to try for sensory grounding is the 5-4-3-2-1 method. This method involves using all of your senses to observe your surroundings.

Here's how it works. Right where you are, make a list of:

- 5 things you can hear
- 4 things you can see
- 3 things you can reach to touch with your hands
- 2 things you can smell
- 1 thing you can taste

This simple exercise is a great way to pull your thoughts away from whatever might be triggering your anxiety and bring you back to the present moment.

Physical Grounding Techniques

Physical grounding techniques are a great way to distract you from what you are feeling by engaging actively with the world around you. By pulling you out of your mind and into your body, physical grounding techniques are a good way to offer yourself an opportunity to calm down and relax when you are feeling on edge or distressed. Here are some physical grounding techniques you can try:

- Submerge your hands in cold water. Focus on the feeling of the cold water on your hands and all the sensations the temperature causes.

- Go for a walk outside barefoot. Being barefoot will help you connect with the different sensations of what you feel beneath your feet. Take note of the sounds you hear, the different animals and insects you see, and the smell of plants and flowers. Try to identify each one.

- Do some exercise, even if it's a few sit-ups and some jumping jacks.

- Listen to soothing music. Music can have a deeply calming effect and help ease feelings of stress and anxiety.

- Take a hot bath. Break out the candles and rose petals if you need to. Allow yourself to relax and soak in the warmth.

Mental Grounding Techniques

Do you have a happy place in your mind that you often go to when you are feeling mentally and emotionally overloaded? This is a great example of a mental grounding technique.

Mental grounding techniques usually involve imagining or visualizing things that will help soothe you and bring feelings of peace and calm. Doing this enables your mind to shift gears and can alleviate your stress response and the resulting symptoms.

Visualization

Much like going to your happy place, visualizing involves filling your mind with images and scenes that will bring about a sense of calm. You can picture yourself walking down the beach with the soothing sounds of the ocean and the feeling of the warm sand between your toes. You could imagine yourself on a remote island somewhere, soaking up the sun and sipping on a cocktail. Choose any scenario you can picture in your mind that will make you feel happy and at peace and can be used as an effective tool for visualization.

Describe a Cupcake

I know this sounds silly, but I can personally attest to the effectiveness of this simple technique. Picture a cupcake in your mind. Describe how it looks and what decorations it might have. Imagine the flavor of how it smells. Think of how it might taste. As you gradually immerse yourself in this visualization, you will find yourself completely distracted from whatever situation was causing you stress or anxiety.

The mind is a powerful tool. By using these techniques to distract yourself and redirect your thoughts and attention to things that make you feel good or happy, you can effectively manage overwhelming thoughts and feelings.

Conclusion

The power of mindfulness strategies is in realizing that you've had all the tools you need to manage and cope with your stress and anxiety inside of you all along. By incorporating these exercises and tools into your daily life, you will experience immense relief from the distressing thoughts and feelings you may be struggling with.

Sometimes, it can even be as simple as closing your eyes and taking a few deep breaths. That's all you need to ground yourself in the present moment and remind yourself to just be where your feet are. When you are consistently rooted in the present, it becomes so much easier to not become engulfed by your fears of the future and all of the uncertainties that have been keeping you up at night.

Learning some easy techniques to handle these feelings when they come up can also prevent them from bleeding into the rest of your day. You can deal with the situation as it happens, process it, and then let it go. Practicing acceptance and observing your thoughts and emotions without judgment is another incredible way to keep your anxiety from getting the better of you.

Progressive muscle relaxation might just be your ticket to kissing goodbye to those chronic pains associated with tension! When you learn not just how to relax but how to differentiate between how your body feels in a relaxed state and when you are stressed and become aware of the areas in your body where you hold the most tension, you can alleviate a lot of the physical discomfort you have been dealing with. Implementing PMR regularly will keep you feeling more relaxed more often and maybe give your clenched jaw a break.

Staying grounded is the best way to keep your thoughts from running away with you. Remember to just be where your feet are. Notice the little things, pay attention to the world around you, and not the chaos going on inside your mind. Now, you have started your collection of stress management tools. You have practical methods to use both in the heat of the moment and as a regular part of your daily routine. So, take a deep breath, visualize your new life, and let go.

Chapter 4:

Healthy Coping Strategies

Coping skills are the tools we use to build up our stress management skills to prevent a freefall into distress. They also help us negotiate with our triggers and mitigate our response if we are triggered. –Faith Harper

Cracking open a cold beer after work is probably something a lot of people can relate to. Whether you experienced it in your home growing up or were exposed to it through watching old-school sitcoms, there's something so stereotypical about a man rewarding himself with a beer after a long day of work. It used to be a part of my routine, too. I'd come home, carrying all the baggage of the stressors of the day, head directly to the fridge, and grab myself a can. Then, I would kick off my shoes, put my feet up on the couch, and catch up on sports news while drinking. That was sometimes the most relaxed I'd feel all day. As time went on, I began to rely on the promise of that cold beer to get me through some of the more difficult days. I'd stare at the clock, counting down the hours until I could go home and unwind with my beer and my sports.

Eventually, I started allowing myself two or three beers on days when I really felt like I was at my breaking point. I'd formed such a strong association with the idea of beer and stress relief that it was the only thing that made me feel better when I was on edge. As time went on, I started to see how this seemingly harmless habit had become somewhat of a crutch for me. Instead of just having a beer to unwind, I'd turned alcohol into an unhealthy coping mechanism to help me manage my stress and anxiety. As a result, I'd failed to develop any other coping skills and was on the verge of creating a very dangerous dependency.

The importance of learning healthy coping skills isn't just to keep you from drowning in your stress and anxiety but also to keep you from falling prey to other more detrimental forms of coping. Knowing how to deal with your feelings in the moment is one thing and definitely a useful skill to have, but having other tools for consistent long-term management is equally important. In this chapter, we'll look at different healthy coping strategies you can begin incorporating into your daily routine. By adopting these skills into your life, you will enable yourself to enjoy more sustainable relief from the effects of your stress and anxiety and be equipped to manage them in a way that no longer impedes your ability to live your life to the fullest.

Engaging in Hobbies and Interests

Do you ever wonder what makes children so happy? Sure, they don't have mountains of bills to pay and a mortgage hanging over their heads, but it's a lot more than that. Children spend the majority of their time doing things they enjoy, as opposed to things they are forced to do. Somewhere along the way, we stop dedicating time to the things that brought us that sense of happiness and wonder, and that's when the stress and anxiety come creeping in.

Making time for yourself to engage in hobbies and interests outside of your formal responsibilities can be a great way to mitigate the draining effects of stress and anxiety. In fact, pursuing your other interests might even improve your work productivity.

Stress and anxiety trigger hormones like cortisol, which is responsible for many of the unpleasant physical symptoms we've discussed. However, when you are doing things that bring you joy and satisfaction, you trigger a different hormone: dopamine. Dopamine is basically your happy hormone; it produces pleasurable feelings and also affects your mood and motivation.

When you do something that makes you feel good, you flood your body with dopamine, which is a great way to counteract stress-related hormones.

Benefits of Hobbies

Pursuing your hobbies and interests is incredibly beneficial not only to your stress and anxiety but also in other aspects of your overall health and well-being. Some of the other benefits you will enjoy include:

- improving your relationships and giving you the opportunity to meet new people

- giving you a sense of purpose and fulfillment

- improving your confidence and self-esteem

- helping keep you fit and physically healthy

- offering you an opportunity to explore your interests and discover your talents

When it comes to stress management, taking the time to enjoy a hobby can help take your mind off your problems. It can also make you feel better about yourself to do something you enjoy and are good at, which will help combat the negative thoughts that come with anxiety. Taking up a social hobby is also a great way to help you with your anxiety, which may have caused you to isolate yourself and limit social interactions.

Overall, hobbies and interests are a deeply fulfilling and productive way to mitigate the negative impact of your stress, not just by stimulating your body to produce dopamine but by giving you something positive to shift your focus to and providing you with a healthy outlet for your emotions.

Pursuing New Hobbies

I know the idea of trying something new probably fills you with anxiety, and you are thinking that's counterproductive—but hear me out. Trying something new can be both thrilling and rewarding. And we've said before that not all stress is bad. Have you ever heard of eustress? Eustress is a form of stress that leads to positive outcomes like resilience, motivation, and happiness. It's like that feeling you get in the pit of your stomach just before you muster up the courage to step out of your comfort zone. A little eustress will go a long way in helping you find new and exciting ways to alleviate your stress and anxiety.

Trying something new doesn't have to mean going from zero to a hundred. You don't need to go to the extreme; you can start small. Sign up for a class you wouldn't usually attend. Join a team for a sport you have seen but never had the opportunity to try. The worst thing that can happen is that you realize it's not for you and decide to try something else. On the plus side, you might just discover something new about yourself by uncovering a talent you never knew you had!

Whether it's cooking, hiking, reading, or skydiving, the positive benefits of trying new things are innumerable. Physical hobbies will improve your mental and physical health by keeping you active. Group hobbies will improve your social connections by giving you the opportunity to interact with people who share your same interests. Technical hobbies will enhance your focus and stimulate you intellectually. Including hobbies in your life also gives you a more well-rounded lifestyle. You won't feel as trapped in the work-life cycle as you did before. Even if it takes you a while to find something that sticks, it will definitely be worth the effort.

Stress Relief Through Creativity

A lot of people shy away from using creative outlets to de-stress because they don't see themselves as being particularly gifted artistically. Well, I have a box full of paintings that look like they were done by a kindergartener that will convince you otherwise. The power of using creativity as a form of stress relief is not in the outcome but in the process. You need to release yourself from the pressure to create something that looks amazing and just create something that feels good. If you are overthinking it, you are doing it wrong.

People have long used creativity as a way to express themselves in ways they can't using words. Whether it's to process a loss or express their innermost desires, art in all its forms has always been a great tool for self-expression. Sometimes, it can feel so therapeutic to slap a bunch of paint on a canvas and just swirl it around until it makes sense or to sculpt an entirely non-functional coffee cup out of clay. When you create, you get to lose yourself in the process. It can feel like a kind of meditation where all other thoughts leave your mind and your focus is completely consumed by what you are creating.

Imagine how relaxed and calm you would be if you set aside an hour a week to simply sit and let your creativity flow. If you could shut out the world for a while and reduce your entire existence to whatever it is you are creating. Well, why not try it out?

Let's look at some fun, creative avenues you can experiment with as a form of stress relief.

Art Therapy

Art therapy has been used in many therapeutic contexts for the treatment of stress and anxiety. Many people struggle to put their feelings into words and find it easier to paint or draw visual representations of their thoughts and feelings. Art therapy is effective whether you do it in an official capacity, in a group setting, or on your own. It allows you to express yourself in whatever way you feel most comfortable and also fosters feelings of calm and relaxation. No matter the medium, creating art is a fun and engaging way to distract your mind from whatever else is going on in your mind. When you are in the process of creating art, your mind releases that happy hormone dopamine, and you will find yourself feeling uplifted. You might also discover that you have a knack for a particular form of artistic expression and that it brings about self-confidence and pride. Even if the result isn't what you expected, you will feel a sense of accomplishment whenever you complete an art piece. Whether you hang it up on your fridge or hide it in a box in your garage, you will always feel a sense of achievement.

Some different forms of art therapy you can try are:

- painting
- sculpting
- photography
- adult coloring books
- doodling or drawing
- scrapbooking
- diamond dot art

Remember, you don't need to be a Monet to paint. Creativity is for everyone, whether you are an expert or a complete novice.

Music

You probably have a playlist full of feel-good music you listen to when you need to hype yourself up or motivate yourself to get things done, or a playlist you play when you are at the gym to keep you from leaving before you have completed all your reps. It should come as no surprise then that music can also be used as a way to relieve stress and anxiety. And not just classical music but anything that makes you feel good can be good for you. When it comes to managing stress and anxiety, music has been known to:

- decrease cortisol levels
- lower your heart rate
- release endorphins (more feel-good hormones)
- reduce stress-related symptoms

However, the benefits of music when it comes to relieving stress and anxiety are not limited to merely listening to it. Actively engaging with music in the form of dancing or creating it is even more effective as a creative outlet for all those uncomfortable feelings.

Movement and Dance

Again, I want to reiterate that being good at dancing is not a prerequisite for enjoying the many amazing benefits movement and dance therapy have to offer! In fact, being skilled has very little to do with the therapeutic value of this form of therapy. The power of movement and dance therapy is in allowing yourself to feel the music and move your body in whatever way best helps you express yourself.

It doesn't need to look like you are a backup dancer for Taylor Swift! Simply allowing your body to flow with the sounds is all you need to feel the happy hormones flowing through you. Choosing a form of dance that resonates with you is just as important as the movement itself. Whether you prefer a dance class like ballet or a more energetic form of movement like Zumba, make sure to select something that really appeals to you. You can even just freestyle to your favorite playlist at home if that's what you are most comfortable with.

Dancing as a form of stress relief also has the added advantages of:

- improving your cardiovascular health
- increasing your energy levels
- relieving tension in your muscles
- giving you better sleep

So, what are you waiting for? Hit play and feel the stress and anxiety drain out of your body with every beat.

Balance Between Work and Leisure

For many of us, finding the right balance has been an elusive goal that we've been chasing for longer than we can remember. Struggling to keep your work and personal life from bleeding into each other can be one of the biggest causes of stress and anxiety. When you fail to create a clear distinction between the two, your life becomes a constant onslaught from both, with neither one ever getting your full attention. It can be so frustrating having to field calls from home while you are at work, being forced to intervene in whatever is going on between the children. Sitting at the dinner table answering work emails can be equally as exhausting. You can end up feeling like you never have time to yourself, never mind the energy required to give either of those aspects of your life your full attention at any given moment.

The thing to learn is that a work-life balance isn't something you find; it's something you create. And how do you do that? I'm so glad you asked! What you are lacking are boundaries. Boundaries are the lines we draw that let people know what we are and are not willing to do. They protect your time and energy and can help keep you from burnout. When you have clear boundaries between work and your personal life, you can stop the endless overlap you are struggling with in your daily life. Setting clear boundaries also enables you to give your full attention to whatever you are doing without being constantly distracted by outside influences.

Setting Boundaries

Setting boundaries isn't easy, especially if you have never had them. Additionally, you might encounter some resistance to them at first, but remember that change takes time. The more you reinforce your boundaries, the more likely it is that people will respect them. When you place boundaries on things like your time and energy, you protect yourself from people taking advantage of you and overextending yourself. Setting boundaries in your relationships is also essential because it allows people to understand how to treat you with respect and what makes you uncomfortable or unhappy.

Work Boundaries

When you set clear boundaries in your professional life, you reduce stress and anxiety by:

- avoiding taking on too many responsibilities

- limiting your workload to what you can reasonably manage

- allowing you to focus on important tasks, increasing your productivity

- having clear expectations on what's expected of you

- facilitating healthy, respectful relationships with your colleagues

Finding the right balance between work and personal life is crucial for managing your stress and anxiety. It's all about setting boundaries that allow us to fully focus on each aspect without feeling overwhelmed. You see, boundaries aren't restrictions; they are tools that help us manage our time and energy effectively. By clearly defining when we're in work mode and when we're off-duty, we can prevent burnout and ensure we have the space to recharge. These boundaries also help us communicate our needs to others, whether it's our colleagues respecting our personal time or our family understanding our work demands. Creating a clear distinction between work and leisure time empowers us to bring our full attention to each role we play without feeling pulled in different directions. It's about creating a routine that supports both our professional responsibilities and personal well-being.

Planning Leisure Activities

Self-care is an important aspect of stress management and reduction of anxiety. This means taking time out away from responsibilities and demands on your time. Putting self-care on your schedule is one of the best ways to ensure you actually make time for yourself. After all, you make time on your schedule for other important things, right? Why not include yourself? Planning leisure activities for yourself allows you the opportunity to recharge and reboot. Work and home life can be so draining, as much as you might love both. When you are constantly giving away your energy, you might find yourself feeling depleted. This only works to exacerbate your feelings of stress and anxiety. Taking the time to focus on yourself is your opportunity to refuel your tank and make sure you are in a space where you can be and give your best. When planning leisure activities, make sure to select things that you enjoy and bring you mental and emotional peace. It's your time to explore your hobbies, find new passions, and spoil yourself a little.

Conclusion

Dealing with stress and anxiety doesn't always need to be turning to a list of "break glass in case of emergency" strategies. It's about more than knowing what to do in the thick of it, although having those tools is always helpful. Developing healthy habits and positive coping mechanisms can be an amazingly proactive way to help you improve your overall quality of life.

By incorporating hobbies and interests that stimulate the production of happy hormones like dopamine in your system, you can give yourself relief from stress and anxiety, as well as boost your overall mood and health. Whether it's rediscovering an old passion or unearthing a hidden talent, finding ways to bring yourself joy and fulfillment outside of your regular work and other responsibilities will bring new dimensions to your life and offer you opportunities to improve yourself in many ways. You might find that you make new friends with similar interests or take up a new sport that will greatly improve your health and vitality.

Expressing yourself through art and music is another incredible avenue you can explore as an outlet for those uncomfortable thoughts and feelings. You can depict your stress in a sculpture or release your anxiety through therapeutic dance movements. The possibilities are limited only by your imagination. Remember that the power of creative expression is in the process, so just allow yourself to fully embrace the journey.

Creating a work-life balance for yourself is about learning to set clear boundaries that protect your time and energy. Placing a clear line between the two prevents them from overlapping and making it impossible to find time for yourself. Remember to schedule self-care as a priority. Making time to recharge yourself will help you regroup and make stress and anxiety less overwhelming when they occur.

So, forget about what others will say about your stick paintings or what they'll think about you attending hip-hop classes. This is your journey and yours alone. Go create, explore, and engage. You never know what you might find along the way!

Chapter 5:

Building Emotional Resilience

Successful people demonstrate their resilience through their dedication to making progress every day, even if that progress is marginal. –Jonathan Mills

A few years ago, I decided to start running. I'd seen people around my neighborhood doing it, and it looked like an easy way to stay fit without the added burden of a gym membership. I was wrong. I took one jog around the block and instantly regretted it. My legs were shaking, and my lungs felt like they were on fire. I couldn't believe there were people out there who actually ran marathons. However, I stuck with it.

Week after week, I laced up my running shoes and took to the streets. I found that, as time went on, my body got stronger. I built up stamina, and my lungs started getting used to the chill of the crisp morning air. I could go longer without needing to stop and pretend to tie my shoelaces because I was so out of breath. After a few months, running became almost second nature to me, and I found myself looking forward to those morning runs, excited to see if I could improve my time or go a longer distance.

I mention this story because emotional resilience is very similar. When you are faced with a stressful situation or something that triggers your anxiety, your immediate reaction might be a bit overwhelming. Maybe you don't have the right tools, or you are not accustomed to being in that heightened emotional state. Learning how to build endurance and stamina comes with practice. Much like with exercising, the first few attempts might leave you drained for days afterward. But as you keep at it, the time it takes for you to recover from these episodes becomes shorter. Resilience is the power to bounce back from these setbacks. Using the right tools and coping mechanisms, episodes of stress or anxiety don't need to leave you feeling emotionally hungover for days and leak into the rest of your week.

You can lace up those emotional regulation techniques, shake off those uncomfortable thoughts, and keep going. In this chapter, we'll explore the concept of emotional resilience. We'll learn not only what it is but also how to build your own. With the right combination of daily habits and coping strategies, you, too, can bounce back stronger than before.

Understanding Emotional Intelligence

You have probably heard about IQ, which is how we measure a person's cognitive intelligence. But academic excellence isn't the only form of intelligence that affects your level of success in life. Actually, intelligence comes in many different forms; one of them is emotional intelligence. Emotional intelligence is your ability to understand and recognize emotions in yourself and others. Additionally, it's how you use that understanding to influence actions and behavior positively. People with high emotional intelligence are able to show empathy, resolve conflict, regulate their emotions, and make healthy, informed decisions.

What Is Emotional Intelligence?

A lot of us are ruled by our emotions. We act without thinking in the heat of the moment because we're driven by our impulses. Emotional intelligence gives you the ability to not allow your feelings to cloud your judgment. You are able to respond to situations instead of reacting to them. You are also capable of regulating your emotions in a way that allows you to bring yourself down from a heightened emotional state so you can address situations in a rational, calm manner. Sounds like a superpower, right? It kind of is—especially when you have lived for so long in a fog of stress-fueled mistakes and anxiety-induced missed opportunities.

The Components of Emotional Intelligence

There are five key components of emotional intelligence:

Self-Awareness

Awareness enables you to acknowledge the role that your emotions play in shaping your actions and decisions, as well as those of the people around you. It's also about understanding how your behavior and actions impact the people around you.

Emotional Regulation

The ability to control and regulate your emotions is vital because your emotions can impact your behavior and decisions. Emotional regulation doesn't mean turning into a robot and ignoring your feelings. It's about finding ways to express them appropriately.

Motivation

People with high emotional intelligence aren't motivated by external rewards and recognition. Instead, they are motivated internally by their purpose and personal goals.

Empathy

Empathy is the ability to put yourself in someone else's shoes and see things from their perspective. It's about not just acknowledging their feelings but being able to understand why a situation has caused them to feel that way.

Social Skills

Social skills like active listening, body language, conflict resolution, and persuasiveness allow you to get along well with others. They enable you to build strong, meaningful relationships and better understand others and yourself.

Emotional Intelligence in Managing Stress and Anxiety

When it comes to managing your stress and anxiety, emotional intelligence is the ace up your sleeve. Developing your emotional intelligence in the five key components above can really give you an effective tool for managing stress and anxiety.

Self-awareness can help you become more attuned to your emotions, making it easier to know when you have been triggered. It can also help you become more proactive in your endeavors to manage your stress in effective ways.

Self-regulation can help you become more flexible, making it easier to cope with and adapt to change and unforeseen circumstances. You will be able to take a step back from your emotions to respond to the situation in a healthy way.

Developing your social skills can help you navigate conflicts without escalating them. Being able to communicate effectively with others and understand their perspectives can reduce stress and anxiety caused by misunderstandings in your relationships and interactions with others.

Emotional intelligence also helps you gain a more positive outlook toward life and stressful situations. When you can see the silver lining instead of drowning in negative thoughts and feelings, it's easier to come up with effective ways to overcome your stress and anxiety. Additionally, it helps foster resilience, which will help you adapt and bounce back from challenges.

How to Improve Your Emotional Intelligence

Building up your emotional intelligence can sometimes feel like an uphill battle—but remember, everyone starts somewhere. The more you practice, the better you will get.

Here are some things you can try to help you along:

- Be more aware of your emotions. Look inward to observe how you feel in different situations and what might be causing those feelings.

- Pay attention to how others feel. Recognize how your words and actions impact how others treat you.

- Treat other people how you would expect to be treated if you were in the same situation.

- Work on your communication skills, learn how to express yourself clearly, and practice active listening.

- Be open to receiving feedback from others on how you can improve and what you need to work on.

- Gain a deeper understanding of your strengths and weaknesses.

- Take accountability for your actions and learn from your mistakes.

By following these steps and integrating them into your life, you can slowly improve your emotional intelligence. This will help you manage your stress and anxiety, improve your relationships, get through conflict amicably, and improve your ability to communicate effectively.

Practicing Gratitude

Have you ever heard of reciprocal inhibition? It's a concept in psychology that says it's impossible for a person to feel two contradicting states simultaneously. In essence, it means that it's impossible for you to feel both stressed and grateful at the same time. That's why practicing gratitude can be an extremely powerful aid in combating stress and anxiety.

Gratitude helps boost your mental and emotional well-being by shifting your perspective from negative thoughts and feelings to positive ones. When you choose to express gratitude in a situation where you are feeling stressed or anxious, you immediately diffuse those overwhelming thoughts of negativity that are playing through your mind.

Gratitude doesn't just have a profound psychological effect, but it has a physiological effect, too. When you practice gratitude, you activate the reward center of your mind, which releases dopamine into your body. That's the happy hormone we spoke about before. So, by simply being grateful, you are altering your brain chemistry to induce positive feelings that will make you feel more positive and uplifted. And it's so much more than that. Getting into the habit of practicing gratitude regularly can actually alter your brain chemistry and strengthen your neural connections. This means that over time, you will effect permanent changes in your brain's chemistry that are very beneficial to your mental well-being.

When you learn to practice gratitude, you teach your mind to focus on the positive aspects of situations, leading to a more positive outlook on life. Finding the good in any situation can help you become happier and more content in your daily life. It can help combat negative thinking patterns and make you more resilient to challenges.

When it comes to building resilience, gratitude can help you shift your perspective from dwelling on the negative impact of situations. By learning to see the silver lining or find the good in bad situations, you allow yourself to become more optimistic and hopeful. When you face challenges with a more positive attitude, it's easier to see the other side of hardships and not become engulfed in them.

Let's look at some of the practical ways you can start incorporating the practice of gratitude into your daily life.

Gratitude Journaling

A gratitude journal is a place where you look back on your day and write down everything you are grateful for. It doesn't have to be anything profound; even the smallest thing, like enjoying the sunshine, is something worth mentioning. We so often dwell on the negative aspects of our days that the things that brought us joy, even for a moment, can completely slip our minds. When you keep a gratitude journal, you remind yourself of everything you have instead of dwelling on what you lack or getting caught up in everything that's going wrong.

Making time to reflect on moments of your day that put a smile on your face reminds you that things aren't as bad as they sometimes seem. Making a habit of looking for the good parts of your day also reframes your thinking. You help your mind shift into a more positive outlook, which can impact how you experience life in general. The more you focus on good things, the more good things you attract.

The practice of gratitude journaling has been known to have tremendous positive benefits, such as:

- increased feelings of happiness
- reduced stress
- improved resilience
- enhanced levels of self-awareness
- heightened optimism

The great thing about gratitude journaling is that starting one doesn't take much effort. All you need is an empty notepad and a pen. Or, for those who are more tech-savvy, you can download an app or write it in your notes. You can write a list of gratitudes every day or once a week; the frequency doesn't matter as long as you are consistent with it. It won't take you a long time to begin seeing the results. You will notice yourself paying more attention to the good things that happen throughout the day so you can put them in your gratitude journal later.

It also encourages you to take note of the smaller things that you usually wouldn't think twice about, like getting a smile from a stranger.

The more you think about it, the more you will realize that you have so much to be grateful for.

Expressing Appreciation

We're all taught it's good manners to say "thank you" as kids. Some of us have gotten so in the habit of saying it that it's lost its meaning. It's more of a knee-jerk reaction than a genuine, heartfelt show of gratitude. However, expressing appreciation goes far beyond just being polite. When you express your appreciation, you make an effort to show people that you value and respect them and their efforts.

Have you ever felt underappreciated by someone? As if nothing you do for them is ever good enough, and they only notice your flaws? I'm sure we can all relate to that feeling of not being valued, and it's not a good one. Sometimes, in our relationships, especially with those closest to us, we fail to express our appreciation because we assume that people know how we feel about them.

Verbally expressing our appreciation to people is an amazing way to practice gratitude. When you tell people that you acknowledge their efforts and value the role they play in your life, it has a positive ripple effect. It not only improves your relationships but also strengthens the bonds you share with them. Everyone loves to feel appreciated, and by showing people that you appreciate their kindness, you encourage further acts of kindness.

When you thank someone, you validate their effort. It's easier to continue showing kindness and compassion to others when you don't feel like your efforts are going unnoticed. And when you feel validated and appreciated, you will feel inclined to spread that joy by showing your appreciation to others. A small act of expressing appreciation can have such a big impact on your environment, cultivating an atmosphere of gratitude not just in yourself but in everyone around you.

Practicing Mindful Thankfulness

Mindfulness and gratitude go hand in hand and, together, are an excellent recipe for emotional resilience and inner peace. We've already explored how gratitude encourages us to appreciate the good things we've experienced, the people we have in our lives, and all our achievements. Mindfulness can further help you cultivate that spirit of appreciation by reflecting on where you are in your life right now. Think of everything you have in this moment—everything you have overcome, everything you have achieved. Think of the people in your life who care about you, the people that you value. Imagine how you would feel if you lost everything and everyone. Doesn't that make you want to be more grateful?

We so often take what we have for granted—as if it will always be there. We put our achievements on a shelf behind us as we reach out, looking toward the next thing we don't have, the next thing that will make us feel happy or fulfilled and content. But mindfulness isn't about what you are aiming for or what you lack. It's about pausing and firmly rooting yourself in this present moment where you lack nothing. If you have shelter, health, food, and security, you already have so much more than many people in the world. That, in itself, is something to be grateful for.

Practicing gratitude in the present is an amazing way to instantly uplift yourself if you find yourself in a dark place. Simply close your eyes for a moment and picture someone you love, someone whose presence in your life you cherish. Next, imagine that person smiling. Imagine them receiving the blessings of everything their heart desires. Hold onto that feeling of warmth. Did you smile? That's how easy it is to be grateful. Mindful thankfulness helps you realize that gratitude is never more than a few moments away.

Developing a Growth Mindset

A lot of your outlook and the way you experience stressors in life depends on your mindset. Naturally, as someone who suffers from anxiety, I always pictured things going wrong. I would automatically imagine the worst outcomes of every situation, and that made me approach challenges with a very negative attitude. When you are always waiting for things to go wrong, sometimes you miss the opportunity to see how things can go right. Sometimes, this negative outlook on life kept me from trying things that could have been incredible opportunities for growth and self-improvement. And I'm sure we all know by now that the only way to ensure failure is not to try at all. If you can relate to these thoughts and feelings, you will benefit from learning how to develop a growth mindset. What's that? It basically embodies everything we've discussed in this chapter so far. It's about choosing to see the positives in life and not letting your emotions, like fear and anxiety, get the better of you. A growth mindset is about seeing challenges as opportunities and mistakes as learning curves.

When you have a growth mindset, you know that you don't just give up when something goes wrong. You take that as a lesson because now you know what doesn't work. A growth mindset also helps you understand that not knowing something isn't an excuse not to try but a chance for you to learn something new.

Building resilience is about more than just not staying down when you take a knock. It's about getting back up with a positive attitude and a determination of spirit that will propel you to keep moving forward. Now, I know this all sounds like a lot, so let's break it down.

Embracing Challenges

Nobody coasts through life. At some point, we're all going to stumble into some sort of obstacle. What makes the difference is how you approach these situations. Are you going to dissolve into a puddle of stress because you are unsure how to proceed? Are you going to listen to your anxiety telling you that you are going to fail, no matter what? Giving in to these thoughts and feelings might be what has held you back in the past. It's time for you to unlearn these behaviors. By simply looking at your challenges as an opportunity to grow, you can rewire the way you view them. A challenge is not an obstacle to your success; it's a stepping stone to your improvement.

Learning From Failures

Everybody makes mistakes. I know that feeling of disappointment can be pretty demoralizing, but you can't let it keep you from trying again. If you are going to fail, fail forward. It's like getting to a dead end on a journey. You just need to circle back and choose a different path. Think of it this way: Every failure takes you one step closer to success.

Believing in Potential

We're all our own worst critics, but your negative beliefs about yourself can be doing you more harm than you know. Believing in your own potential is one of the hallmarks of the most successful people. Sometimes, your belief that you can do something is the only thing that will keep you going when all indicators point in the other direction. Even if you need to fake it until you make it, just tell yourself that you can, and eventually, you will believe it.

Conclusion

Your mind is a powerful tool—one you can use to either build yourself up or break yourself down. Stress and anxiety can sometimes make you feel like you are not entirely in control of your thoughts or feelings, like you are a servant to your impulses and negative perceptions. Cultivating the skills inherent in emotional intelligence can help put you firmly back in the driver's seat. Learning to recognize, understand, and control your emotions is incredibly liberating and empowering. It will not only improve your mental well-being but will have a positive impact on your interactions and relationships with the people around you.

Having an attitude of gratitude is like putting on a pair of rose-colored glasses every morning before you step out into the world. Training your mind to focus on the positives and acknowledge your blessings will make you feel happier and more content. Turning gratitude into a habit and not just a chore will completely shift your perspective in life. You will start learning to appreciate what you have instead of focusing on what you lack. And don't forget to express your appreciation out loud because not everybody knows just how much you love and cherish them. Even if they do, it's always nice to hear.

Being resilient is a combination of so many things, but a lot of that depends on your mindset. Developing a growth mindset is the final piece to your armor of emotional resilience. Once you are in control of your emotions and have learned how to see the good in every situation, you also need to see the good in the hard times.

Building resilience is about knowing that you have the emotional strength to overcome challenges, acknowledging that there is a silver lining to every cloud, and realizing that failure is not a death sentence. With all three of these tools in your arsenal, you will be unstoppable.

Chapter 6:

Lifestyle Changes for Stress Reduction

> *Doctors won't make you healthy. Nutritionists won't make you slim. Teachers won't make you smart. Gurus won't make you calm. Mentors won't make you rich. Trainers won't make you fit. Ultimately, you have to take responsibility. Save yourself.* –Naval Ravikant

Stress and anxiety are so much more than an uncomfortable feeling that ruins the rest of your day. They affect you mentally and physically and impact every aspect of your life. Nothing is safe from its clutches, from your career to your relationships and even your thoughts. Knowing this, you must approach managing your stress and overcoming your anxiety from every possible angle. We have already explored different ways to alleviate it, from shifting your mindset to adopting healthy coping mechanisms. We have also learned various strategies you can use in the heat of the moment that can help you diffuse those overwhelming emotions.

In this chapter, we'll be discussing lifestyle changes. Believe it or not, there are certain habits you can incorporate into your daily routine that will make your life less stressful and leave you less susceptible to anxiety. There are so many things you do that are probably greatly contributing to your stress and anxiety. Many habits have become so ingrained that you probably don't think twice about doing them. I didn't even realize how much my daily routine was harming me until I started changing my lifestyle. I was shocked by the massive changes I saw in myself; I couldn't believe it!

Something as simple as replacing the soda I had at lunch with a bottle of water ended up having such a big positive impact. It had a knock-on effect on the rest of my dietary choices, which, up until that point, I had never even bothered to suspect had anything to do with my anxiety and stress levels. Some lifestyle changes can be a lot more difficult, such as quitting smoking. But if you really commit yourself to doing everything you can to reduce the burden that stress and anxiety have placed on you, it's definitely worth the effort.

Lifestyle changes can be challenging, even the small ones. Remember that it takes up to 30 days to make or break a habit. That means, through consistency and perseverance, you'll eventually reach a point where making these healthy lifestyle choices becomes second nature. And, trust me, your mind and body will thank you.

Importance of Balanced Nutrition

You probably already know how important a good diet is for your body to function properly. If you didn't have it drilled into you as a child, then you learned the hard way when you couldn't concentrate in class because you'd skipped breakfast. However, eating a balanced diet does more than just give you energy and keep your organs working; it also affects your mind.

Have you ever been hangry? Hangry is what happens when you get cranky because you haven't eaten. You might feel more irritable than usual and lash out at people for no reason. If you know this feeling, you know firsthand how your diet can directly affect your mind. The first step to managing stress and anxiety is to eat properly. This means not skipping meals and making sure your food has enough nutrients and vitamins to give you enough energy for the day.

When you skip meals, you risk having low blood sugar. Low blood sugar can trigger feelings of anxiety and cause stress. Without enough energy, your mind and body won't be able to cope with the effects, and you'll be in a very uncomfortable position. To avoid this, make sure you're eating every three to five hours.

A balanced diet includes all of the major food groups, these are:

- fruits
- vegetables
- dairy
- grains
- protein

Protein doesn't necessarily mean meat; you can get protein from many other sources. What's important is that you include a good variety of all five food groups in your daily food intake. Eating a healthy combination of food is a great place to start when it comes to giving yourself a strong foundation for your overall well-being. However, you can also eat specific foods that will help reduce your stress and anxiety.

Foods That Lower Stress and Anxiety

Certain foods have been found to reduce stress or improve anxiety symptoms. This is because they contain chemicals that lower cortisol levels, induce relaxation, improve blood flow, and aid in the production of serotonin. Adding these foods to your diet can do wonders for relieving stress and anxiety symptoms and improving overall mental well-being.

Some of these foods are:

- oily fish (like salmon, herring, and mackerel)
- fermented foods (like miso, kombucha and sauerkraut)
- leafy greens (like spinach, kale, and Swiss chard)
- foods that are high in vitamin B (like beef, chicken and eggs)

- foods that are high in magnesium (like avocados, bananas, and dark chocolate)

- foods that are high in protein (like almonds, lentils, and quinoa)

Many of these foods have anti-inflammatory properties that help reduce the amount of cortisol in your body. They also have a relaxing effect that can help reduce the symptoms associated with anxiety. Remember that adjusting your diet for stress reduction is a marathon, not a sprint. This means you'll see the improvements over time and with consistent effort. Shoving an entire slab of dark chocolate in your mouth before a board meeting isn't going to quell your anxiety!

Foods to Avoid

Much as there are foods that lessen stress and anxiety, there are also foods that make them worse. Certain types of food can actually spike cortisol levels in your body or have other negative effects on your system. For example, eating food that is high in sugar can cause an imbalance in your blood sugar levels, which will lead to a sudden dip. When your blood sugar drops unexpectedly, it can trigger or worsen your symptoms.

Some foods you should try and avoid are:

- foods with processed sugar

- caffeine

- alcohol

- foods containing simple cards (like cakes and pastries)

Starting your day with a cup of coffee can be an incredibly difficult habit to break, but caffeine can actually induce anxiety. Perhaps instead, you can try starting your day with a refreshing smoothie. Fruits such as pears, apples, bananas, and citrus fruits have all been linked to having stress-reducing qualities.

Hydration

It doesn't matter if the glass is half empty or half full—drink it! Dehydration has been proven to have a strong link to the symptoms of stress and anxiety. Since we're made up mostly of water, our bodies view dehydration as a threat to our survival, thereby triggering our stress response. Dehydration also triggers other symptoms which will only exacerbate feelings of anxiety.

Without enough water, our bodies aren't able to function properly. This means simple things like being able to concentrate and complete basic tasks become harder and seemingly impossible. Dehydration also negatively impacts your body's ability to handle stress, and you might find that simply drinking a glass of water makes a big difference in how you're feeling.

How much water is enough water? That depends on your age and fitness level. On average, it's recommended that women drink about 9 cups of water a day, and men drink about 12 cups. It sounds like a lot, but if you get into the habit of sipping regularly, you'll find it's not as intense as if you sit and try to fill your quota just before bed.

For those of us who are a little forgetful, there are apps you can download onto your phone that send out a notification at regular intervals reminding you to drink water. You can space these notifications throughout your day in a way that's most convenient for your schedule. As you get into the habit, you'll find that you don't need the reminders as much.

Regular Physical Exercise

We all know the health benefits of regular exercise, but how many of us actually make time for it? When you're already feeling the pressure of deadlines and a hefty workload, it can seem like taking a few minutes to go for a scenic walk is a waste of time. However, it is quite the contrary. Exercising doesn't just benefit your body, but also your mind.

Remember those happy hormones we spoke about? When you're active, your body releases endorphins. These account for that feeling they call a "runner's high," but any form of exercise can induce feelings of euphoria. In addition to uplifting your mood, regular exercise makes your body more resilient to some of the physical symptoms of stress and anxiety. It strengthens your heart and helps release the tension in your muscles. Even just five minutes of aerobic exercise a day has been shown to decrease the physical symptoms associated with anxiety.

Since exercising mimics the physiological effects of stress, you're actually teaching your body how to work through these feelings when they arise in a less intense scenario. Exercising can also be cathartic. It distracts your mind from all the stressors of the day and gives you something outside of yourself to focus on for a while. People often turn to exercise as a way to clear their minds because it has such a meditative effect.

Incorporating exercise into your daily routine can improve your mood, boost your immune system, help you release tension, and relieve some of the mild symptoms of anxiety. With all this in mind, it's no wonder it's been so highly recommended as a part of any effective stress management regimen.

Here are a few tips to get you started on your fitness journey:

Start Small

You're not going to become an Olympic athlete overnight, so don't go in guns blazing. Start by introducing an easy form of exercise into your routine and see how you manage that. You can always increase the length and intensity as you go along; however, when you're getting started, it's important to ease your way in.

Make It Fun

The best way to motivate yourself to exercise is to do something you enjoy. You're less likely to do it if it's not something that interests you. Exercising is about more than pumping weights at the gym; anything that gets your body moving and your heart pumping can be used as exercise. This can be doing sports or taking up an active hobby. When you exercise by doing something you like, it's easier to stay consistent and stick with it.

Stick With It

I've said this before, but if you want to see results, you need to be consistent. It will feel odd at first, and you might drag your feet, but eventually, you will get used to it. Make sure you do it regularly and not only when you feel like it. If it helps, schedule physical exercise in your planner; that way, you will hold yourself accountable to make sure you follow through.

Set Goals for Yourself

Another great way to keep yourself motivated is to set goals. Building up a routine and getting into the habit is beneficial, but you also want to see results. Running around the block every week is great, but you should either challenge yourself to improve your pace over time or extend your run's length. Setting goals will give you a sense of accomplishment when you reach targets and is also an excellent way to measure your progress.

Sleep Hygiene

As someone who has suffered from stress and anxiety, I know all too well the impact it can have on your sleep. If, like me, you know exactly how many tiles are on your roof, I'm sure you are desperate for ways to help you get more sleep. Feelings of stress and anxiety can become heightened at night, causing trouble either falling or staying asleep. This is because those final hours of the evening are usually the quietest for most people.

Lying in bed at night is probably the first time all day that you haven't been focused on the next task, appointment, or concern. As you start winding down, your mind starts firing up, filling your thoughts with all the intrusive thoughts you have spent all day trying to keep at bay. With all those worries and anxieties filling your mind, sleep can prove to be quite elusive. Thankfully, there are things you can try to help calm down your mind before bed and make it easier for you to fall asleep.

Starting the day in a sleep deficit leaves you at a massive disadvantage. Our minds use sleep as an opportunity to recharge for the next day. Sleep is also essential for the proper functioning of your body's systems. When you don't get enough sleep, you increase your risk of developing medical conditions like high blood pressure, diabetes, Alzheimer's, and obesity.

Most adults don't get nearly enough sleep, as experts suggest we need between seven to nine hours every night. If you are falling dismally short of this, you are not alone. But let's figure out a way to start fixing that.

So, what is sleep hygiene? No, it has nothing to do with brushing your teeth before bed, although that's also a good idea. Sleep hygiene refers to the healthy habits, behaviors, and other environmental factors that contribute to you getting a good night's sleep. Contrary to what you may believe, a good night's sleep doesn't start the moment your head hits the pillow. You need to put habits and routines in place leading up to bedtime that can help ensure your mind and body are in the right state to rest.

Good Sleep Hygiene

Setting the stage for sleep is essential. You can help yourself by introducing habits and creating an environment that will help your mind and body relax. This includes things like:

- Maintain a consistent set time for going to sleep and waking up—yes, even on the weekends.

- Start preparing for sleep an hour before bed by winding down.

- Avoid using electronics like your phone and laptop while you are in bed.

- Keep the lighting in your bedroom to a minimum, and get blackout curtains if necessary.

- Take a warm bath or a hot shower.

- Set your room temperature to be on the cooler side.

- Avoid eating or drinking anything from three hours before bedtime.

- Limit any intake of caffeine or alcohol.

- Don't exercise just before bed.

- Calm your mind using meditation, breathing exercises, or journaling.

Once you start setting these measures in place, you will start seeing a difference in your sleep patterns. I didn't realize that scrolling through social media in bed wasn't a good way to keep me distracted when I couldn't sleep; it was actually a part of the problem! The light from your electronic devices can interrupt your circadian rhythm. That's the part of your brain that regulates your sleep cycle and releases the hormones that tell your mind it's time for sleep. By turning off all your devices an hour before bed, you will already be taking a huge step toward improving your sleeping habits in the future.

Avoiding Harmful Substances

We all have our vices. Not everyone is born brimming with healthy coping mechanisms and a natural sense of well-being. It's likely you might have picked up some unhealthy habits along the way as a way to cope with your stress and anxiety. Some of these might not be helping you the way you thought they were, and others might be doing you more harm than good. The thing about using harmful substances as a way to deal with your stress and anxiety is that these quick fixes prevent you from looking for healthier, more sustainable ways to manage your symptoms. That's in addition to the other harmful effects they're likely causing you.

Nicotine

With the number of people who use nicotine products as a way to cope with stress and anxiety, you would probably be surprised to find out that nicotine has been proven to worsen these conditions. As much as lighting up a cigarette can temporarily give you a feeling of relief, in the long term, it will make your symptoms so much worse.

What nicotine does is release a small amount of dopamine in your brain, giving you the illusion that it's alleviating your stress and anxiety. Underneath this, however, it's causing your body more stress by inducing physiological changes such as:

- accelerating your heart rate
- increasing your blood pressure
- constricting your blood vessels
- tensing your muscles
- limiting the amount of oxygen available to your brain

You may not notice these effects immediately, but once the dopamine hit wears off, you will ultimately find yourself feeling more stressed than you did before you smoked.

One of the symptoms of nicotine withdrawal is anxiety, which will probably trigger you to want to smoke more to alleviate this, and so begins the vicious cycle.

Alcohol

Alcohol is yet another substance that produces temporary euphoria but ultimately leaves you feeling worse off. Alcohol alters the chemicals in your brain and affects the levels of serotonin. As a result, you will find that your symptoms of stress and anxiety come back worse than before once the alcohol begins to wear off.

In addition to this, heavy drinking has a multitude of adverse effects on your overall health, including your brain, liver, and heart. Using alcohol as a coping mechanism will take a toll on your health, not to mention having to deal with the horrendous hangover!

The temporary relief you may enjoy in the immediate aftermath of smoking or drinking isn't worth the ultimate toll they're going to take on your health, both physically and mentally. Letting go of these habits isn't easy, but it's certainly something worth doing for the sake of your long-term well-being.

Conclusion

Many of us are oblivious to how our daily habits can potentially be contributing to our stress and anxiety. After all, the last thing you are thinking about when ordering a pizza is the possibility of it negatively impacting your mental health, right? But your diet does impact your stress. So, make sure you are making good dietary choices that align with the rest of the positive changes you are making to your life. I'm not saying you need to turn vegan overnight and start only buying organic foods, but being mindful of what you eat is a great first step. Staying hydrated is also something you need to be aware of, and if you need an extra reminder, there's an app for that!

Physical exercise isn't something you can do only in a gym. Find something you enjoy doing and make that your regular form of exercise. That way, it will feel more like a hobby than a chore. Your relationship with sleep up until this point has probably been a frustrating one. Thankfully, you now have some great tips on how to create a more conducive sleeping environment for yourself. Sleep is essential for your mind and body to recharge; you don't want to start the day on low battery.

The quick fix offered by harmful substances can be alluring at first, but think of the long-term impact they're having on you. Remember, when you turn to these substances as a crutch, you are preventing yourself from learning how to stand on your own two feet.

Managing stress and anxiety is a multifaceted endeavor, and you will need to focus on making consistent changes in every aspect of your life if you want to reap the benefits. Luckily, many of these changes come with a whole lot of other great benefits for your overall well-being. So try not to take everything so seriously; just do your best. Eat right, get moving, drink water, and get a good night's sleep. You have earned it!

Chapter 7:

CBT Techniques

It isn't what you have, or who you are, or where you are, or what you are doing that makes you happy or unhappy. It is what you think about. –Dale Carnegie

Along my journey in self-empowerment and transformation, I often found myself stumbling over old habits. As much as I was, and still am, determined to adopt healthier, more positive habits and behaviors, I still made mistakes. Every now and then, I would find myself falling back into old behaviors and ways of thinking. It was almost as if I would reset to my default settings—and those settings included things like negative self-talk and other toxic thought patterns that impeded my ability to enact positive changes.

It was then I realized that as important as learning new habits is, sometimes it's just as important to unlearn the old ones. Before I could effectively implement my new tools, I first had to diffuse the old ones. I had to remove the power they had over me so they couldn't stand in the way of my progress.

Once I'd learned this, it was like I was starting on a clean slate. Sure, I'd still slip up now and then, but it wasn't the same as before. I could now defend myself against the negative effects of my old habits while simultaneously working to integrate the new ones.

In this chapter, we'll explore some helpful cognitive behavioral therapy techniques. With these techniques, you will learn ways to combat old ways of thinking whenever they arise. You will recognize and identify the unhelpful thought patterns that have been holding you back and empower yourself to overcome them.

Challenging Negative Thoughts

We've all fallen prey to negative thoughts at one point or another. As humans, we're hardwired with a negative bias. This means we have a natural tendency to focus more on negative things or be more deeply affected by them. That's probably why it's so much easier to remember your mistakes than your achievements. Silencing that inner critic is not only possible, but it's necessary for the sake of your continued growth and mental peace. Sure, in small doses, it can be helpful, especially when that voice is encouraging you to try harder or warning you against something that might not end well. But it can become very damaging when it's just a broken record pointing out all of your shortcomings. Before we learn the tricks of overcoming these thoughts, let's explore them a little further.

Types of Negative Thinking

You might find yourself falling into the trap of several forms of negative thinking. Knowing how they manifest will make it easier for you to become more aware of them when they pop up.

Black and White Thinking

When you see things in extremes without taking into account the many gray areas that can exist in any situation, we say you are using black-and-white thinking. An example of this is if you see yourself either as a complete failure or a roaring success in regard to a particular scenario. This kind of thinking doesn't allow you to see the lessons in your failures or the points of improvement in your successes. Seeing life through this lens can be extremely detrimental to your growth.

Jumping to Conclusions

Sometimes, we think we're psychics the way we assume we know how things are going to turn out. By jumping to conclusions, you can sometimes create a self-fulfilling prophecy for yourself, especially when the assumptions you have made are negative.

Catastrophizing

It's good advice to hope for the best and prepare for the worst, but always assuming the worst is going to happen is unhealthy. When you automatically assume that the worst is going to happen in any situation, you are placing an unrealistic expectation of the future. In reality, things are never actually that bad, and you have caused yourself added stress and anxiety unnecessarily.

Overgeneralizing

When you take the outcome of a previous experience and assume any similar situation you face in the future will end in the same way, you are applying overgeneralizing. Yes, we need to learn from our mistakes, but when you go into a situation already thinking you know how it's going to end, you miss out on the opportunity to learn new ways of doing things. You are also causing yourself more stress and anxiety by telling yourself that your efforts won't affect the outcome, as if it's inevitable.

Labeling

When you give yourself negative labels, you put yourself into a box that constricts your ability to grow. For example, by labeling yourself as someone who isn't good at sports, you deprive yourself of the opportunity to learn. And you are putting yourself in a position where any situations involving that skill will trigger your stress and anxiety.

These are just a few of the negative thinking patterns that can affect you. The popular term for these thinking patterns is cognitive distortions because they have the power to distort your reality. The danger with these thoughts is that your thoughts are very influential on the way you experience life overall. Thoughts can influence your emotions, which, in turn, affect your behavior. When you are constantly stuck in negative thinking patterns, it has a domino effect on other aspects of your life. It can negatively impact your relationships, career, and mental and physical well-being. That's why it's vital to get it under control. These are not just harmless self-criticisms; their impact is anything but.

So, what can you do to change these thoughts? You can start by seeing them for what they are: thoughts. They are not facts, and you shouldn't treat them as if they were. When you can simply observe these thoughts instead of internalizing them as truth, you are already one step closer to overcoming them.

Cognitive Reframing

Cognitive reframing is exactly what it sounds like: It's about changing the way you think. Now that you are more easily able to identify negative thought patterns, you can learn how to stop them from negatively impacting you.

Cognitive reframing is about analyzing the thought and then changing it to better suit reality. Next time a negative thought comes up, don't just accept it as truth or try to push it aside; take the time to analyze it.

Ask yourself the following questions:

- Is this true?

- Are these thoughts based on facts or feelings?

- What evidence is there to verify these thoughts?

- What can I do to influence this situation?

- Am I underestimating my ability to handle this situation?

When you take a step back and actually challenge these thoughts, you will find that many of them are not based on factual evidence but rather imagined scenarios you have created in your mind. Often, cognitive distortions can blow small things out of proportion, and when you really stop and think about it, the situation isn't as intense as you thought it was. Now that you have identified the thought and analyzed it, the next thing you need to do is replace it. When you replace the negative assumption with something more aligned with reality, your outlook on the situation might completely change.

Let's use an example: You have had a disagreement with your partner, and they've said you need to talk. Automatically, you decide that your partner is going to break up with you.

Cognitive reframing says first, you need to identify this thought as being negative. You are falling into the negative thought pattern of jumping to conclusions or catastrophizing. You don't know for certain that your partner is going to break up with you. You are not a mind reader or a psychic, so you can't assume to know what your partner is thinking or what their intentions are. Next, we need to question the validity of the assumption. Surely, you have had disagreements before. They didn't result in a breakup, so why would this time be any different? It's more than likely your partner simply wants to discuss the issue so you can come to some sort of agreement and make peace.

By following these simple steps, you have deescalated a situation from working yourself up into a frenzy to a more manageable state of anxiety over resolving a conflict. This is cognitive reframing in action. Try it for yourself next time a negative thought comes up; you will be surprised how effective it can be.

However, it's important to note that when you replace your thoughts, they should be replaced with something realistic. If you swing from one extreme to the next, you might set yourself up for failure or disappointment. For instance, don't go from assuming your partner is going to break up with you to telling yourself that they're about to propose. That wouldn't be helpful or realistic! Reframing isn't about going from negative to positive, although some optimism wouldn't hurt. It's about going from negative to realistic. When you have a more realistic outlook on the future, you will be better prepared for whatever may come.

Positive Affirmations

You have probably heard a lot about positive affirmations and how effective they can be at increasing your confidence and self-esteem. After years of beating yourself up mentally, you could probably use a little bit of kindness. That's what positive affirmations are. It's about replacing that endless loop of self-criticism that was constantly playing in your head with some encouragement and acknowledgment of your positive traits.

Knowing the power of negative thoughts will probably help you appreciate and understand the benefits of positive affirmations a lot more. You will probably feel a bit silly at first, but trust me, you will get used to it.

Positive affirmations don't need to be grandiose or complex. You can start with basic things like:

- "I am capable."
- "I am strong."
- "I am worthy."

Try using just a few words that signify the place you would like to be mentally and emotionally. When you affirm yourself in this way, you cultivate a more positive sense of self. Instead of focusing on your flaws and ruminating over your mistakes, you give yourself the opportunity to appreciate the person you are. You are training your mind to look for the good in yourself, which will bring more of it out.

Just like we spoke about how practicing gratitude will refocus your mind to see the positive aspects of your day, positive affirmations will refocus your mind to see the positive aspects of yourself.

Behavioral Activation

Earlier, I mentioned that your thoughts, feelings, and behaviors are all interlinked. Behavioral activation functions on that premise. If we can use our thoughts to influence our emotions and change our behaviors, then surely it could work in reverse, too, right?

Behavioral activation is about engaging in behaviors that will alter your emotions and therefore influence your thoughts. Sounds complicated? Let's explore it further.

Redirecting Your Thoughts

Behavioral activation can reduce stress or anxiety by redirecting your energies and attention, for example, by doing things that you enjoy when you are feeling stressed. Let's say you are under a lot of pressure at work, and you are obsessing about a big project you need to get done. You are probably telling yourself that you will never finish on time, and then your boss will fire you. These thoughts can become so overwhelming that you can't think of anything else.

So, you take a break from work to go and work in the garden. At first, your mind is still obsessing about the project. But, as you actively engage in an activity you enjoy, it triggers pleasurable feelings, which eventually begin to change your state of mind. Now, the project doesn't seem as disastrous as it did a moment ago. Suddenly, you are able to conceptualize new strategies for tackling it that you hadn't even considered before. You finish with a pristine garden bed and a more relaxed state of mind. This is how behavioral activation works.

Replacing Bad Habits

Behavioral activation can also be used to curb some of those harmful or unhealthy coping mechanisms you might have developed over time. By replacing the habit with something healthier and more beneficial, it's easier to overcome it. If you are used to having a drink every time you feel stressed, your body is going to crave that same sense of release every time that stress is triggered. If you just sit on your hands doing nothing, you are more likely to give in to the temptation. Instead, try to replace the drink with something healthier that will still give you the same feeling. Go outside and hit the punching bag for a few minutes. Soon, your mind will associate stress relief with that habit instead of the old one.

Improving Your Relationships

Stress and anxiety can make you want to isolate, and as a result, your relationships suffer. You don't want to go out as often, or you don't make as much of an effort to keep in touch with your loved ones. This isolation can worsen your feelings because you now have more time to sit alone with them. By making an appointment or scheduling time every week to go out with your friends or visit a loved one, you are pulling yourself out of that tendency. You will probably find that you end up enjoying your time with them and feel a lot less tense afterward. Sometimes, you just need to physically force yourself to do something before you realize how much you really need it.

Many of the strategies and techniques we've discussed so far all centered around ways for you to think your way into a new way of behavior, but sometimes that isn't always possible. In those cases, you might need to try and behave your way into a new way of thinking.

Conclusion

Stinking thinking can be a massive stumbling block when it comes to trying to adopt healthier coping mechanisms. Sometimes, it feels like your inner critic is holding you back from a lot of things. As much as you can do your best to practice mindfulness and other positive coping strategies, your negative bias will get the better of you if you don't learn how to manage it.

Challenging negative thoughts is the best way to overcome negative thinking patterns. When you confront these thoughts and analyze their validity, you will find that most of them are based on cognitive distortions. Reframing and turning them into something more realistic is the best way to diffuse them. Remember, don't overdo it on the positivity because going from one extreme to the next is setting yourself up for disappointment.

When you are at your wit's end trying to get out of your head, and nothing else seems to be working, perhaps it's time to try some behavioral activation. By using your behavior as a way to influence your thoughts and behavior, you might find it easier to bring yourself down from an emotionally heightened state. Whether you just need a break from your obsessive thoughts, are fighting the urge to turn back to an old vice, or simply need a friendly face and a hug, behavioral activation is an effective tool to guide you through those situations.

Cognitive behavioral therapy is based on techniques that help you use the connection between thoughts and behavior to make the changes you need to live a fulfilling life. Now that you have learned how to silence your inner critic, don't forget to practice some positive affirmations. Show yourself a little kindness and remind yourself that you've got this!

Chapter 8:

Social Support and Communication Skills

You can't achieve anything entirely by yourself. There's a support system that is a basic requirement of human existence. To be happy and successful on earth, you just have to have people that you rely on. –Michael Schur

You have probably heard it said that no man is an island, and it is true. As much as we all want to believe that we are independent and capable of looking after ourselves, the truth is that we need people. When we are low, we need someone to lend us an empathetic ear and help us pick ourselves up again. When we have reached a milestone, we need people to celebrate with us and share in our accomplishments. Yes, you can get through these things alone, but life is just better with people. If you are stubborn like me, you probably hate reaching out to others for help, even though you are always the first one to be there for everyone else. Realizing that I didn't need to face my struggles with stress and anxiety alone was a relief once I'd swallowed my pride and accepted that I wasn't coping.

Even if you don't rely on others for emotional support, just having other people to give you a different perspective or offer some helpful things they tried when they were in a similar situation can make all the difference. Sometimes, it's enough to know that you are not alone in this, that others have been where you are and made it out on the other side.

A big obstacle I discovered when I finally decided to open up about my struggles was my inability to communicate effectively. It's crazy, given how much we communicate with other people in our lives, that we can reach a point where we realize people are receiving a different message than the one we're trying to convey. The frustration this caused almost made me abandon the whole idea of reaching out in the first place. But learning how to communicate effectively is a vital part of this journey. Being confident in your communication skills can help lessen a lot of your stress and anxiety, particularly in social settings.

In this chapter, we will explore the importance of a strong support system around you. Even if it is only one or two people, knowing there is someone in your corner will make this journey a lot less daunting. We are also going to discuss how you can work on your communication skills to ensure that you are properly heard when you open up about your situation.

Benefits of Social Connections

Social support is essential for many reasons. Since we are social beings by nature, a lack of social interactions can have dire consequences on our overall well-being. When it comes to managing stress and anxiety, knowing there are people you can lean on during difficult times can help relieve a lot of the burden of your stressors. Whether it's a friend you can vent to, a therapist who can offer guidance, or a parent who can relieve you of some of your responsibilities for a short while, being able to offload some of what's weighing you down can no doubt be a huge benefit in times of crisis.

However, social connections are beneficial not only during times of stress or anxiety. In general, having a strong support system around you can greatly improve your overall quality of life, your health, and your happiness.

Types of Social Support

Support comes in different forms. Depending on your needs and expectations, you might find yourself utilizing more than one form of social support. Let's look at the three main types of social support:

Emotional Support

Emotional support is the support we get from the people closest to us. This can be your romantic partner, close friends, and family members. When people give us emotional support, they allow us to feel heard and validated in our feelings and experiences. Even if they don't understand what we're going through, they let us know that we don't need to go through it alone. Knowing that you can pick up the phone when you are feeling overwhelmed and call someone who cares about you and is willing to listen can be such a relief when you are feeling on edge. Sometimes, just knowing you have that safety net is enough to dull the feelings of stress and anxiety.

Emotional support can also be received from a support group in a casual or therapeutic session. Being in a space where you can share your thoughts and feelings without judgment can offer comfort and reassurance.

Informational Support

Informational support is a type of support you would receive from your mentors, therapist, or any other professional in the field who has a wealth of knowledge on managing stress and anxiety. These people would be able to offer you advice and guidance for your situation, as well as some practical strategies on how to cope in a healthy way. They may also be able to provide you with resources you can use to aid in managing these thoughts and feelings.

When you feel like you are at a loss as to how you are going to move forward, having someone who knows more about your condition and can offer you effective ways to deal with it can help you feel more in control of the situation.

Instrumental Support

Instrumental support is when people do tangible things to alleviate your stress or anxiety. This can come in the form of helping you financially or offering other resources to facilitate your ability to overcome the stress. For example, if you are stressed because your car broke down, instrumental support can come in the form of either paying for the repairs or giving you a lift to and from work until you can get it fixed yourself.

Instrumental support can come from your close friends and family members or even be offered by your community resources.

Building a Support Network

If you are looking for ways you can build a strong support network for yourself, here are some things you can try:

- Join a support group.
- Rekindle old friendships.
- Find an online community.
- Sign up for a class.
- Attend events.
- Volunteer in your community.

Making new connections and meeting new people isn't easy, but it's an important part of your growth. The more you put yourself out there, the higher your chances of meeting people you can connect with and relate to. Even just the practice of regularly going out can be enough to curb those feelings of loneliness and isolation, leading to reduced stress and anxiety.

Importance of Social Support

No matter the situation you are facing, you can always benefit from reaching out for support. People with a strong support system are less prone to stress because they know that no matter what they're facing, there are people around them who care and are willing to help. Knowing that you don't need to shoulder all of your burdens alone can also greatly reduce those anxious thoughts and feelings and all those sleepless nights imagining the worst-case scenario.

People with a sound support system lead happier, healthier lives. That's because the people around you act as a buffer for stress and a sounding board for your problems. Having friends is important, but being a friend is just as important. Sometimes, just being there for someone else can take your mind away from your own problems for a while.

Having the support of others around you during times of stress can bolster your ability to bounce back, making you more resilient. The advice and coping mechanisms you learn from them can also help you manage these situations better in the future.

Effective Communication Techniques

Have you ever paused to think how many arguments and disagreements you could have avoided with clear communication? Misunderstandings are the source of so much conflict in our lives, from forgetting whose turn it was to take out the trash to not understanding the task your boss asked you to complete. Effective communication isn't only about exchanging ideas and information with other people; it's about doing so in a way that both people understand and are understood and leave satisfied with the result.

A lot of the time, we're so focused on getting our own point across that we don't take in what the other person is saying. This can be a big factor in miscommunication—when two people are talking *at* each other instead of *to* each other. If you want to communicate more effectively, you need to give as much attention to what the other person is saying as you would like them to give to you. When both people are making a concerted effort to see things from the other person's perspective, it's much easier to come to an agreeable resolution to any conflict.

Communication is also not only about words. A lot of what people communicate is conveyed nonverbally through their body language. Learning how to read these nonverbal cues is an important skill if you want to become more effective at communicating. When we're stressed or anxious, we tend to give off very negative body language or incorrectly interpret the body language of others. That's why it's important to never try to address issues when we're in a heightened emotional state; we risk making matters worse. Instead, take a moment to pull yourself together so you can approach the situation calmly and rationally.

The 5 C's of Communication

There are several factors that define what we call effective communication. These factors are collectively known as the 5 C's. When communicating with people, it's important to make sure that what you are saying is:

- clear
- complete
- correct
- concise
- compassionate

Making sure that what you are saying has at least several of these factors is a good indicator that you are communicating effectively. Anxiety can cause you to ramble on in a desperate attempt to make sure people are hearing what you are saying, but truly, less is more. The more short and to the point what you are saying is, the better it will be received. It's also important to consider your audience and deliver your message in a way that is as polite and empathetic as possible if you want others to respond well to it.

Active Listening

One of the most essential tools for effective communication is active listening. This means you don't just hear what the person is saying but do your best to understand it and the underlying feelings behind their words. Like any skill, active listening gets better the more you practice it.

Active listening makes it easier for you to be empathetic toward the other person by fully appreciating their perspective. When you engage in active listening, you are better able to understand what the other person needs or wants from you, reducing the chances of misunderstandings.

Here are some tips for how you can begin practicing active listening in your daily interactions with others:

- Be fully present in the conversation and focus on the person speaking.

- Try not to interrupt, and don't make the conversation about you.

- Show interest in what the other person is saying.

- Listen without judgment, and don't offer advice or opinions unless asked.

- Pay attention to their body language.

When you engage in active listening, you build trust within your relationships and strengthen the bonds you share with others. When people feel heard and understood, they feel validated. This makes it easier for them to feel comfortable communicating with you in the future. You create a space where people feel safe to be vulnerable and authentic, which can only foster an atmosphere of positivity and encourage healthier interactions between yourself and others.

Seeking Professional Help

As much as we all want to empower ourselves to overcome these things on our own, sometimes the most empowering thing you can do is admit that you need professional help. Seeking professional help in the form of a counselor, therapist, or any other kind of medical professional is nothing to be ashamed of. Thankfully, the stigma that was once associated with people who sought the help of therapists has slowly eroded and given way to a generation of people who understand the importance of prioritizing our mental health.

Needing that little extra push or helping hand is not a sign of weakness. It's quite the opposite. It takes a lot of guts to admit when it's time to call in the big guns. As incredibly helpful as self-help strategies and techniques can be in helping you manage your stress and anxiety, sometimes what you need is a more targeted and individualized approach. Perhaps there's a particular situation that you can't seem to wrap your head around, and you feel a therapist can help you process it better.

A licensed therapist with years of experience working with people who suffer from stress and anxiety has a wealth of knowledge to offer. They can also create a personalized treatment plan based on your specific needs and what aligns with your personality and coping styles.

Therapy can also offer you a safe space to air your grievances without fear of judgment. Sometimes, it helps to have someone completely removed from our lives weigh in and give us an objective opinion. Confidentiality also makes it easier for you to be vulnerable and honest, knowing that you will neither be judged nor condemned for your actions.

Some forms of anxiety can't be meditated away and may require additional treatment in the form of medication. If you feel like your anxiety has reached a point where it's making it nearly impossible for you to function, perhaps this is an option you might need to consider. No matter the reason, asking for help is never a bad thing.

Support Groups

As an extension of your therapeutic process, you might also consider joining some support groups. Support groups are an excellent place for you to meet and connect with like-minded people who are facing the same struggles as you and can understand and empathize with what you are going through.

Support groups are also a safe space with no judgment where you can go to share your personal experiences as well as hear the experiences of others. There are many benefits to joining a support group.

Different Perspectives

Being in a support group offers you the opportunity to see your stressors from the perspectives of others. Someone else might give you a different view than the one you initially had on something they may have experienced before themselves. This fosters an environment of shared learning.

Coping Strategies

In a support group, people often share the various coping strategies they may have found effective in their own stress management journey. This gives you a whole new pool of resources to draw from that you can try and implement in your own life. There's the added incentive of knowing they have successfully worked for someone else, and you can always go back to that person for advice and guidance as well.

Encouragement and Validation

Being in a room of people who understand exactly what you are going through can be a powerfully validating experience. Having them hold your hand through your struggles and pat your back when you overcome challenges can give you an extra layer of confidence you didn't even know you needed. Support group members also often hold each other accountable for their growth, and you might find it helpful to have people around you who actively encourage you not to stagnate on your journey.

Conclusion

Self-reliance isn't all it's cracked up to be. We all need people, especially with the mounting weight of pressure modern society has placed on all of our shoulders. Nobody needs to carry their burdens alone. When you build a strong support system around you, you are giving yourself the ability to allow others to help you navigate the minefield of stress and anxiety before it overwhelms you. Accepting that you can't do this alone is the first step toward realizing that you don't have to.

There are people in your life who care about you and genuinely want to help you—so let them. Support, whether emotional, informational, or tangible, is never wasted. Knowing you have a safety net to fall back on should you need it is sometimes enough to keep you from falling at all. So often, we're stressed because we think we need to do everything ourselves, but thankfully, we don't.

Effective communication will strengthen your relationships and help you avoid conflicts based on misunderstandings and miscommunication. Remember that communication is about understanding not just what the other person is saying but why they're saying it. Engaging in active listening is a great skill to practice if you would like to improve your communication skills because it will teach you how to listen to understand and not to respond.

Needing professional intervention is nothing to be ashamed of. Placing your mental well-being ahead of your pride is admirable. Sometimes, you need a more targeted approach to stress and anxiety than you can create for yourself, and that's okay. What is important is that we get better, not how we get better. Joining a support group is also an incredible way to acquaint yourself with people who understand what you are going through.

A support group can be a therapeutic, safe space where you can share your experiences, listen to and learn from others' experiences, and even form connections that will bolster your support system.

Help is always available, and resources are endless. There's no reason for you to suffer in silence or try to go it alone. You would be surprised how many people are able and willing to offer you support; all you need to do is ask.

Chapter 9:

Overcoming Fear and Worry

One can choose to go back towards safety or forward towards growth. Growth must be chosen again and again; fear must be overcome again and again. –Abraham Maslow

A life ruled by fear and worry can be incapacitating. A healthy level of fear is normal, and we've spoken about how this survival mechanism can keep you from putting yourself in danger or give you that little extra bit of motivation to get things done. But when your mind becomes a minefield of terrifying possibilities for the future, fear is unbearable. Seeing the worst-case scenario in every situation can leave you trapped, like a prisoner in your own mind. Our natural instinct is always to avoid fear, to turn and run in the other direction. However, avoidance is neither effective nor sustainable as a coping mechanism. The best way to overcome your fears is to face them head-on. It is only when you tackle them that you realize they're probably not as bad as you thought.

It's like when you were a child and pictured there was a monster under your bed. The more you obsessed with the idea, the worse it became. You imagined all manner of horrendous creatures silently lurking in the shadows. The thoughts probably kept you up at night, mistaking every sound you heard or shadow you saw as proof of this fantasy. Do you remember how relieved you felt when your parents made you look under the bed to assure you there was nothing there?

You might have even laughed at yourself for how far your mind had gone to convince you of something that was never real. A lot of your fears operate on the same premise. The longer you entertain the idea, the more it snowballs into something that can seem insurmountable. The only way you will keep them from overwhelming you is to force yourself to stop running and hiding from them. You need to find the courage to look under the bed and confront the truth.

In this chapter, we'll be exploring the nature of fear and how it manifests in your life. We'll be tackling ways you can start beating those worries by facing them head-on instead of allowing them to escalate and overwhelm you.

Understanding the Nature of Fear

You already know that fear is a natural, primal response to a real or perceived threat to danger. It triggers both a physical and emotional response. The physiological response to fear is pretty universal. We all experience the same physical reaction of the fight or flight response. However, our emotional responses to fear are unique to each person. Fear triggers some of the same parts of your brain as the emotions of happiness and excitement. For this reason, we can sometimes find the experience of fear to be positive, for instance, when watching a scary movie or going through a haunted house. To some, they find the physiological response thrilling and love the rush of adrenaline. These are the kinds of people who enjoy extreme sports like skydiving or bungee jumping. They associate the physical fear response with something positive, and so it has a positive effect on them. Others, especially those who suffer from anxiety, experience fear as something incredibly negative. Anxious people avoid any people or situations that they think might trigger their fear response.

Causes of Fear

As much as fear is primal, it can come in various forms. The three different causes of fear are:

Instinctual

This is the fear triggered by your inherent need for survival. It can be in response to a real or perceived danger and is probably the most familiar form of fear.

Learned

A learned fear is a fear that results from a traumatic experience. We adopt this fear to protect us from facing similar situations in the future. Learned fear can be of people, places, or scenarios that we have created a negative association with based on previous experiences.

For example, if you have been in a car accident on the highway, you may develop a fear of highways or driving in the aftermath of that event.

Taught

Societal and cultural influences can also be the cause of some of your fears. Say, for example, you grew up in an unsafe neighborhood; you might fear going to certain parts of that area or have learned to feel anxious around people who fit a type of stigma associated with criminal activity.

The great thing about a fear that has been learned or taught is that it can be changed. By examining the root of these fears and assessing their validity, you can dispel many of these feelings. Say, for example, you feel anxious around people who are heavily tattooed. By simply getting to know someone in this demographic, you can realize that they're also just people and probably don't all fit the stereotype you have come to believe they do.

Effects of Fear

Fear can have a devastating effect on your life and daily functioning. Some fears can hold you back in life. Some of these are the fear of things like:

- the future
- rejection
- loneliness
- the unknown
- failure
- change
- judgment
- inadequacy

The biggest downfall of fear is that it dictates your actions. Common responses to fear are fight, flight, faint, or freeze. In these situations, your behavior comes from a place of being emotionally overwhelmed as opposed to being a rational choice based on your well-being or the best course of action in a given scenario.

When you act based on fear, you are likely to miss opportunities due to avoidance mechanisms or isolate yourself from others. Remember the monster under your bed? Fear can make things seem a lot worse than they are. When experiencing life through this lens, even inconspicuous things can feel catastrophic. When you are scared, everything is scary. For example, if you are afraid of losing your job, everything your boss says to you can be misconstrued as criticism and a cause for dismissal. Even if your boss just points out a minor mistake you have made, in your mind, you see that as grounds for your immediate dismissal. As you can imagine, living this way can make life unbearable.

Embracing Your Fears

Acceptance is probably the last thing you consider doing when it comes to dealing with fear. Our natural responses to fear are usually avoidance, denial, resistance, or distraction. However, none of these courses of action will help you solve the problem. Facing your fears isn't about beating them but about accepting them. Practicing the mindfulness techniques we've explored will aid you in taking a step back from the fear and viewing it in a non-judgmental way.

When you can observe your fear instead of indulging in it, you will be able to understand it better. You can ask yourself where this fear stems from, what's been triggering it, and how it's been dictating your decisions and influencing your behavior. And then you can accept it. Accepting doesn't mean letting it run rampant in your life, but allowing it to be a part of you without negatively impacting your life.

The best way to deal with fear when it comes up is to:

- acknowledge
- accept
- accommodate

When you acknowledge the fear, you are already taking a huge step forward from your previous instincts to avoid, deny, or deflect. You can become aware of the fear and accept that this is how you are feeling. Next, you can accommodate it by coming up with a positive way of processing it without leaving a negative impact. By acknowledging, accepting, and accommodating our fears, we learn beneficial strategies for dealing with them. Accommodating a fear can be anything from sharing our feelings with someone we trust, mindful breathing exercises, or journaling about our feelings. Anything that can help you allow the fear without suppressing or acting out on it. When you have these tools in place, fear no longer becomes a source of anxiety or dread. Instead, you can experience it like any other unpleasant emotion you need to process and release.

Exposure Therapy

Repeated exposure to similar situations can create a sense of familiarity, decreasing the fear response that those situations trigger. This premise is the basis upon which exposure therapy functions. The idea is that by repeatedly putting you in situations where you are forced to face your fears head-on, you can gradually become desensitized to them, drastically reducing the fear associated with them.

Benefits of Exposure Therapy

Exposure therapy can be hugely beneficial for anyone whose fears are limiting their ability to live a full life. For example, if you have a fear of flying, that's causing you to miss out on business opportunities. Sometimes, the discomfort of having to overcome your fear is a small price to pay in comparison to the relief and other advantages of removing it as an obstacle.

Some other benefits of exposure therapy are:

- helping you understand the source of your fear

- helping you replace the instinctual reaction with more realistic thoughts

- reducing the intensity of your reaction to the fear

- allowing you to understand that your assumed outcomes are not based on reality

- showing you that you are capable of withstanding your fears

- giving you an opportunity to see that your fear is not a danger to you

Exposure therapy has been proven to be effective in treating fear and anxiety, as well as phobias and other types of anxiety disorders. By allowing yourself to be exposed to your fears, you are empowering yourself to realize that you can and will survive them.

Types of Exposure Therapy

Exposure therapy is conducted in many different ways, and the success of each method largely depends on the person, what they're comfortable with, the nature of the fear, and the severity of their fear. You are obviously not going to treat a fear of venomous snakes by locking someone alone in a room with dozens of them!

Exposure therapy can be tailored to suit various fears, ensuring its effectiveness in helping you confront your specific challenges. By gradually introducing you to feared stimuli in a controlled environment, exposure therapy aims to alleviate the anxiety associated with it and desensitize you to the triggers that once caused distress. Different techniques can be used, such as virtual reality exposure, systematic desensitization, and flooding. The structured approach aims to guide you through confronting your fears in small steps, allowing you to gradually experience increasing levels of discomfort and anxiety in a safe setting. Repeated exposures diminish the initial distress associated with the fear as you learn to cope with your emotions and reactions more effectively.

Virtual Reality Exposure Therapy

Thanks to advancements in technology, you can now face your fears head-on from the comfort of your couch. In virtual reality exposure therapy, individuals immerse themselves in computer-generated simulations that replicate real-world scenarios related to their fear. This method provides a controlled environment for individuals to confront their fears in a safe and manageable way, allowing them to practice coping strategies and gradually reduce their anxiety levels.

By engaging with virtual scenarios that trigger their fear response, individuals can learn to regulate their emotions and behaviors in a supportive setting. Virtual reality exposure therapy offers a realistic yet customizable approach to confronting fears, helping individuals build confidence and resilience in facing their anxieties.

For example, if you fear flying and are afraid of having a meltdown on a plane, this would be an amazing way for you to face that fear while still subconsciously knowing that you are still firmly on the ground. Instead of holding an entire plane hostage and demanding an emergency landing because you can't take anymore, you can put yourself on the plane virtually. This will help you acclimate to the real-world experience without the added fear of your reaction.

Systematic Desensitization

Systematic desensitization involves creating a fear hierarchy, ranking situations from least to most anxiety-provoking, and systematically being exposed to these scenarios in order of severity. You would start at your lowest fear and slowly work your way up. By starting with the least anxiety-inducing situation and gradually moving toward the most feared scenario, individuals can acclimate themselves to increasing levels of fear and discomfort. This gradual exposure allows you to build tolerance to your fears over time, reducing the intensity of their emotional response and promoting a sense of control over their reactions. Systematic desensitization empowers individuals to confront their fears in a structured and supportive environment, fostering emotional resilience and adaptive coping strategies.

An example of this would be if you have a fear of flying. You would start by simply talking about flying. Then, you would look at a picture of a plane. Slowly, you would build up to the actual experience, getting closer with each session.

Flooding

Flooding is an intensive form of exposure therapy where individuals are directly exposed to their most feared stimulus until the anxiety response diminishes. By immersing individuals in the feared situation without the possibility of escape, flooding aims to extinguish the conditioned fear response through prolonged exposure. While initially overwhelming, flooding can rapidly reduce anxiety levels as individuals confront their fears head-on and experience a decrease in the intensity of their emotional reactions over time. This approach challenges individuals to directly face their fears without avoidance or safety behaviors, promoting a sense of mastery and control over their anxiety.

Of course, this method isn't a go-to for everyone. As much as it can be incredibly effective, sometimes the risks in a given situation aren't worth the potential benefits. I wouldn't recommend trying this one at home!

Conclusion

Fear is a complex, powerful emotion that can shape our lives in significant ways. It can feel incapacitating, at times driving us to make decisions based on irrational thoughts and feelings. By acknowledging our fears, we take the first step toward understanding and eventually conquering them. Avoidance and denial only serve to reinforce our fears, trapping us in a cycle of anxiety and stress. Through acceptance, we open the door to introspection and growth, allowing us to confront our fears head-on with a newfound sense of resilience and clarity.

By accepting our fears, we develop a deeper sense of compassion and empathy for ourselves and others. This newfound self-awareness empowers us to navigate life's challenges with grace and resilience, transforming our fears into sources of strength and wisdom.

Through exposure therapy, you can begin to transform your relationship with fear and anxiety, cultivating resilience and empowerment in the face of challenges. By embracing controlled exposure to feared stimuli, you can gradually desensitize yourself to triggers that once may have caused you overwhelming distress. Whether through virtual simulations, systematic desensitization, or flooding, exposure therapy offers a structured and evidence-based approach to confronting fear and anxiety. By engaging with your fears in a safe and supportive environment, you can develop the skills and confidence you need to overcome your anxieties and live more fully without the limitations imposed by fear.

Conclusion

Here we are, standing on the precipice of your transformation. This may be the end of this particular part of our journey together, but I hope that, for you, it signifies the beginning. May the skills you have learned and the tools you have gained allow you to embark on an incredible process of self-discovery. They say that knowledge is power, and I believe that the information you have gleaned regarding your stress and anxiety will empower you to finally regain control of them and no longer allow them to infringe on your ability to live life to the fullest.

Self-awareness is the foundation of your new perspective, so cultivate it. Connect with your body so you can know when you are being triggered. Understand how stress and anxiety affect you physiologically so you can start managing your symptoms. Don't ignore the physical manifestations of your stress and anxiety; they are your body's primal response to triggering situations. Instead, use these sensations to learn more about your triggers, your environment, and yourself. Identifying your triggers is the first step toward taking your power back. Once you know the situations that will likely induce these feelings, you can be better prepared to handle them.

Keeping tabs on your stress is as easy as downloading an app or investing in a wearable device. Technology has made managing and reducing your stress so much easier. You can get real-time readings of your physiological responses to stress using apps and devices. From tracking your heart rate to measuring fluctuations in your temperature, technology can be an amazing ally. Conducting daily check-ins or keeping a stress journal are also helpful ways to gain a deeper understanding of your stress and anxiety. By taking the time to reflect, you will be able to spot patterns you might not have seen before, assess your reactions to certain situations, and prepare yourself with better ways to handle those situations in the future.

Don't forget to be mindful. Be where your feet are, and try your best to remain rooted in the present moment. When you do this, you release yourself from obsessing about the future or stressing about the past. Incorporating mindfulness practices like meditation, breath awareness, and body scanning can provide an added buffer for times when your thoughts and emotions may become overwhelming. Remember to use the tools we explored, like progressive muscle relaxation and grounding techniques, whenever you are in a bind. Taking five minutes to calm down will save you from lashing out or making irrational decisions based on your emotions.

Challenge yourself to pick up a paintbrush instead of a beer next time you need to unwind. Taking the time to pursue hobbies and interests outside of work is a fantastic way to give yourself another outlet for those uncomfortable thoughts and feelings. If moving makes you happy, don't let the fact that you have two left feet stop you from signing up for a salsa class! You don't need to look good or be good; it just needs to make you feel good!

Finding the right balance between work and leisure might feel like an exercise in futility, but it's really not. Prioritize yourself and start setting firm boundaries to protect your peace. Developing emotional intelligence is the key to building resilience. Consistency in your efforts to improve things like emotional regulation or social skills is the only way you will see lasting change, so stick with it.

You are never too good to be grateful. Even at your worst, there's something you have that you can appreciate, so find it. When you cultivate an attitude of gratitude, you are training your mind to focus on the positive. As a result, your general outlook will shift from a problem-based view to a more realistic or even optimistic view. Life may not change, but the lens through which you view it can make all the difference.

Speaking of perspectives, I hope you have begun making the shift to a growth mindset. Your belief in your ability to do something might have more influence over the outcome than your actual ability. You need to believe you can do it, or at the very least that you can learn. See your obstacles as opportunities for growth and your mistakes as learning curves. Don't dwell on your failures but on the lessons you can take from them to help you the next time you try. Always remember that a challenge is not an obstacle to your success; it's a stepping stone to your improvement. Be aware of how the foods you are putting into your body affect you. Eating a nutritious diet isn't just about getting in all your food groups; it's about giving yourself the energy you need to cope in stressful situations and manage the symptoms of your anxiety.

It's also about avoiding things that can worsen your symptoms, like caffeine and alcohol. Pick up a fitness activity that doesn't fill you with complete dread and start doing it regularly. Your body and mind will thank you. Overcome your stinking thinking and negative thought patterns by standing up to the bully in your head. Turn those self-deprecating monologues into positive affirmations and reframe your negative perceptions by giving them a healthy dose of reality. Thoughts and feelings are not facts, so don't treat them as such.

Sometimes, it's not so much what you say as how you say it. So, keep working on those communication skills. Practice active listening and watch your relationships flourish—not to mention all the unnecessary conflicts you will be avoiding by doing so.

Nourish the connections you share with the people in your life because they're the ones who might help carry you through the darkest times. Reach out when you need support because we all do at some point. You don't need to be a lone wolf, so find a pack you can rely on. Use your resources, and don't be ashamed if you need a little extra help. Your mental well-being is more important than your pride.

The tools and resources we've learned together are the fuel you need to get you going, but they're useless unless you implement them. Make an effort to start making small changes in your daily routine—changes that align with your desire to live a life that isn't ruled by fear and anxiety or hampered by stress. You can overcome fear and learn to cope with anxiety, and honestly, you deserve to. We don't know what the future holds, so let it go. Stay present, stay grounded, stay grateful, and stay hydrated. Remember that you are not alone, and you don't need to face this alone. You are one step closer to mastering anxiety and stress management. You have all the tools you need—now use them!

References

ADAA. (2023, July 21). *Exercise for Stress and Anxiety | Anxiety and Depression Association of America, ADAA*. Adaa.org. https://adaa.org/living-with-anxiety/managing-anxiety/exercise-stress-and-anxiety

American Psychological Association. (2021). Anxiety. *American Psychological Association*. https://www.apa.org/topics/anxiety/

Ayers, H. (2024, May 17). *Relieve Stress with Creativity Therapy*. UF/IFAS Extension Orange County. https://blogs.ifas.ufl.edu/orangeco/2024/05/17/relieving-stress-with-creativity-therapy/

Badosa, H. (2023, October 9). *Alleviating Impact: How Social Hobbies Can Help Anxiety*. Hobbiesblog.com. https://hobbiesblog.com/how-social-hobbies-help-anxiety/

Bailey, A. (2024, January 24). *What Is Progressive Muscle Relaxation?* Verywell Health. https://www.verywellhealth.com/progressive-muscle-relaxation-5225381

Bernstein, A. (2021, May 21). *40 Awesome Quotes About Stress and Anxiety To Get Rid Of*. Quotes Muse. https://www.quotesmuse.com/quotes-about-stress-and-anxiety/

Bradley, J. (2023, May 22). *The Connection Between Gratitude and Resilience: Building Inner Strength*. The Fresh Writes.

https://medium.com/thefreshwrites/the-connection-between-gratitude-and-resilience-building-inner-strength-c5645d65c0df

Bullock, G. (2017, March 15). *Present-Moment Awareness Buffers the Effects of Daily Stress*. Mindful. https://www.mindful.org/present-moment-awareness-buffers-effects-daily-stress/

Burns, S. (2023, February 26). *7 Tips For Improving Emotional Intelligence (EQ) - New Trader U*. Www.newtraderu.com. https://www.newtraderu.com/2023/02/26/7-tips-for-improving-emotional-intelligence-eq/

Carnegie, D. (n.d.). *Empowering CBT Techniques Quotes: Words of Wisdom for Personal Growth and Cognitive Mastery | Grouport Journal*. Www.grouporttherapy.com. https://www.grouporttherapy.com/blog/cbt-quotes

Cherney, K. (2014a). *Alcohol and Anxiety: Causes, Risks and Treatment*. Healthline. https://www.healthline.com/health/alcohol-and-anxiety

Cherney, K. (2014b, September 24). *12 Effects of Anxiety on the Body*. Healthline. https://www.healthline.com/health/anxiety/effects-on-body#Central-nervous-system

Cherry, K. (2023, December 31). *5 Key Components of Emotional Intelligence*. Verywell Mind. https://www.verywellmind.com/components-of-emotional-intelligence-2795438

Chopra, D., & Sehgal, K. (2017, September 15). *Science Shows How Creativity Can Reduce Stress*. Entrepreneur. https://www.entrepreneur.com/living/science-shows-how-creativity-can-reduce-stress/300347

Clancy, N. (2024, February 12). *Not Drinking Enough Water Is One of the Worst Things You Can Do When Stressed—Here's Why*. Real Simple. https://www.realsimple.com/health/mind-mood/stress/hydration-for-stress

Collins, D. (2021, July 12). *Can Listening to Music Reduce Stress? Research, Benefits, and Genres*. Psych Central. https://psychcentral.com/stress/the-power-of-music-to-reduce-stress#best-genres-for-stress

Cox, J. (2022, June 9). *How to Sleep When Anxiety Is Keeping You Awake: 5 Tips*. Psych Central. https://psychcentral.com/anxiety/how-to-sleep-with-anxiety#anxiety-and-insomnia

Cuncic, A. (2018). *Change your thoughts, reduce your social anxiety*. Verywell Mind. https://www.verywellmind.com/what-is-cognitive-restructuring-3024490

Cuncic, A. (2024a, February 12). *7 Active listening techniques for better communication*. Verywell Mind. https://www.verywellmind.com/what-is-active-listening-3024343

Cuncic, A. (2024b, June 18). *6 Ways to Deal With Negative Thoughts*. Verywell Mind. https://www.verywellmind.com/how-to-change-negative-thinking-3024843#toc-identify-your-negative-thoughts

Dorwart, L. (2022, June 10). *Stress vs. Anxiety: What Are the Differences?* Verywell Health. https://www.verywellhealth.com/stress-vs-anxiety-5323888#toc-triggers-of-stress-vs-anxiety

Duggal, N. (2018, July 13). *What Is Emotional Intelligence and Its Importance | Simplilearn*. Simplilearn.com. https://www.simplilearn.com/emotional-intelligence-what-why-and-how-article#tips_for_improving_ei

Eugene Therapy. (2021, February 11). *5 ways to challenge negative thoughts*. Eugene Therapy. https://eugenetherapy.com/article/5-ways-to-challenge-negative-thoughts/

Fritscher, L. (2023, April 11). *The Psychology of Fear*. Verywell Mind; Verywellmind. https://www.verywellmind.com/the-psychology-of-fear-2671696

Fry, A. (2017, January 19). *The Best Ways to Relieve Stress So You Can Sleep Soundly*. Sleep Foundation. https://www.sleepfoundation.org/sleep-hygiene/how-to-relieve-stress-for-bedtime

Greene, G. (2017). *Stress Management | Internal And External Stress*. Uhc.com. https://healthlibrary.uhc.com/content/healthlibrary/uhc/hl/wellness/stress_management/relax_101/0475_3C_internal_and_external_stress.html

Gupta , S. (2021, June 29). *What Is Exposure Therapy?* Verywell Mind. https://www.verywellmind.com/exposure-therapy-definition-techniques-and-efficacy-5190514

Gupta, S. (2023, November 30). *What Is Chronic Anxiety?* Verywell Mind. https://www.verywellmind.com/chronic-anxiety-symptoms-causes-and-treatment-5272111

Harper, F. (2023, September 6). *Top 21 Coping Skills Quotes (+FREE Worksheets)*. https://ineffableliving.com/coping-skills-quotes/

HealthCentreNZ. (2024, January 28). *The Role of Social Support in Stress Management: Building a Strong Network | Health Centre NZ*. Healthcentre.nz. https://healthcentre.nz/the-role-of-social-support-in-stress-management-building-a-strong-network/

Herrity, J. (2023, February 27). *9 Tips To Improve Your Emotional Intelligence*. Indeed Career Guide.

https://www.indeed.com/career-advice/career-development/how-to-improve-emotional-intelligence

Holland, K. (2018, May). *What Triggers Anxiety? 11 Causes That May Surprise You.* Healthline; Healthline Media. https://www.healthline.com/health/anxiety/anxiety-triggers#triggers

Hoshaw, C. (2022a, January 31). *How Conscious Breathing Can Help Relieve Anxiety and Stress.* Healthline. https://www.healthline.com/health/mind-body/conscious-breathing#what-is-it

Hoshaw, C. (2022b, March 29). *What mindfulness really means and how to practice.* Healthline. https://www.healthline.com/health/mind-body/what-is-mindfulness#what-it-is

Jelinek, J. (2021, July 12). *Mindfulness and Gratitude: Why and How They Should Pair.* Psych Central. https://psychcentral.com/blog/how-gratitude-and-mindfulness-go-hand-in-hand#gratitude

Jovanovic, T. (2018, November 15). *What Is Anxiety?* Anxiety.org. https://www.anxiety.org/what-is-anxiety

Keiling, H. (2022, February 4). *Emotional Intelligence: Definition and Examples.* Indeed Career Guide. https://www.indeed.com/career-advice/career-development/emotional-intelligence

Khoddam, R. (2023, January 11). *Grounding Techniques for Trauma and Anxiety | Psychology Today United Kingdom.* Www.psychologytoday.com. https://www.psychologytoday.com/gb/blog/the-addiction-connection/202301/grounding-techniques-for-trauma-and-anxiety

Lancer, D. (2017, March 3). *Causes of Anxiety Disorders | Psych Central.* Psychcentral.com. https://psychcentral.com/anxiety/causes-of-anxiety-disorders

Langshur, E. (2021, November 1). *How to Make Gratitude a Daily Habit.* Mindful. https://www.mindful.org/how-to-make-gratitude-a-daily-habit/

Laurence, E. (2020, December 9). *Tracking Stress Is the New Tracking Steps.* Well+Good. https://www.wellandgood.com/wearables-that-track-stress/

Legg, T. J. (2018, June 1). *The Basics of Stress.* Healthline. https://www.healthline.com/health/stress#symptoms

Linder, J. N. (2019, June 29). *Mindfulness and Gratitude | Psychology Today.* Www.psychologytoday.com. https://www.psychologytoday.com/intl/blog/mindfulness-insights/201906/mindfulness-and-gratitude

Link, R. (2017, December 31). *11 Signs and Symptoms of Too Much Stress.* Healthline. https://www.healthline.com/nutrition/stress-symptoms#section5

Marks, H. (2023, October 8). *Stress Symptoms.* WebMD. https://www.webmd.com/balance/stress-management/stress-symptoms-effects_of-stress-on-the-body

Maslow, A. (2023, March 31). *85 Quotes On Overcoming Fear That Will Inspire Bravery.* https://theenemyofaverage.com/quotes-on-overcoming-fear/#:~:text=%E2%80%9CYour%20biggest%20fear%20is%20also%20your%20biggest%20opportunity

Mayo Clinic. (2018, May 4). *Anxiety disorders.* Mayo Clinic; Mayo Foundation for Medical Education and Research.

127

https://www.mayoclinic.org/diseases-conditions/anxiety/symptoms-causes/syc-20350961

Mayo Clinic. (2022, August 3). *Exercise and stress: Get moving to manage stress*. Mayo Clinic. https://www.mayoclinic.org/healthy-lifestyle/stress-management/in-depth/exercise-and-stress/art-20044469

Mills, J. (2023, May 31). *71 Best Resilience Quotes for Bouncing Back*. Good Good Good. https://www.goodgoodgood.co/articles/resilience-quotes

Morin, A. (2020, January 28). *Top 10 Fears That Hold People Back in Life | Psychology Today*. Www.psychologytoday.com. https://www.psychologytoday.com/us/blog/what-mentally-strong-people-dont-do/202001/top-10-fears-hold-people-back-in-life

Morin, K. (2023, September 2). *The Importance of Seeking Professional Help for Social Anxiety*. Katy Morin. https://www.socialanxietyantidote.com/blog/seek-professional-help-for-social-anxiety

Mosunic, C. (n.d.). *18 grounding techniques to help relieve anxiety*. Calm Blog. https://blog.calm.com/blog/grounding-techniques

NHS. (2021). *Stress - Every Mind Matters*. Nhs.uk; NHS. https://www.nhs.uk/every-mind-matters/mental-health-issues/stress/

NIH. (2019). *Anxiety & Smoking*. Smokefree.gov. https://smokefree.gov/challenges-when-quitting/cravings-triggers/anxiety-smoking

Nunez, K. (2020, August 10). *Progressive Muscle Relaxation: Benefits, How-To, Technique*. Healthline.

https://www.healthline.com/health/progressive-muscle-relaxation#how-to-do-it

O'Bryan, A. (2022, February 8). *How to Practice Active Listening: 16 Examples & Techniques.* PositivePsychology.com. https://positivepsychology.com/active-listening-techniques/#skills

Pattemore, C. (2021, October 26). *The 6 Best Foods to Help with Anxiety (And Some to Avoid).* Psych Central. https://psychcentral.com/anxiety/foods-that-help-anxiety#seeking-help-for-anxiety

Patterson, E. (2022, April 14). *Does Alcohol Reduce Stress? Link Between Anxiety And Drinking.* GoodRx. https://www.goodrx.com/health-topic/alcohol/does-alcohol-reduce-stress

Pharoan, V. (2023, August 15). *40 Trigger Quotes To Take Charge Of Emotions & Reactions – The Random Vibez.* https://www.therandomvibez.com/trigger-quotes/

Pietrangelo, A. (2017, June 5). *The Effects of Stress on Your Body.* Healthline. https://www.healthline.com/health/stress/effects-on-body#Sexuality-and-reproductive-system

Pradeepa, S. (2023, November 6). *Importance of Saying Thank You: The Power of Appreciation.* Www.believeinmind.com. https://www.believeinmind.com/mindset/importance-of-saying-thank-you/

Psychology Today. (2019). *Mindfulness* . Psychology Today. https://www.psychologytoday.com/us/basics/mindfulness

Purvis, M. (2024, July 22). *Stages Of Stress: How Stress Progresses | BetterHelp.* Www.betterhelp.com.

https://www.betterhelp.com/advice/stress/stages-of-stress-how-stress-progresses/

Ravikant, N. (2023, June 25). *213 Inspirational Positive Healthy Living Quotes -.* https://www.quotestoolbox.com/healthy-living-quotes/

Raypole, C. (2019, May 24). *Grounding Techniques: 30 Techniques for Anxiety, PTSD, and More.* Healthline. https://www.healthline.com/health/grounding-techniques#physical-techniques

Raypole, C. (2023, March 29). *Physical Symptoms of Anxiety: What Your Body May Be Telling You.* Healthline. https://www.healthline.com/health/physical-symptoms-of-anxiety#anxiety

Reid, S. (2023, March 2). *Social Support for Stress Relief.* HelpGuide.org. https://www.helpguide.org/articles/stress/social-support-for-stress-relief.htm

Rice, A. (2021, September 13). *Challenging Negative Thoughts: Helpful Tips.* Psych Central. https://psychcentral.com/lib/challenging-negative-self-talk#how-to-stop

Robinson, L., Segal, J., & Smith, M. (2024, February 5). *Effective Communication.* Help Guide. https://www.helpguide.org/articles/relationships-communication/effective-communication.htm

Scott, E. (2006, April 21). *How to Relieve Stress With Art Therapy.* Verywell Mind; Verywellmind. https://www.verywellmind.com/art-therapy-relieve-stress-by-being-creative-3144581

Scott, E. (2011, January 10). *The Importance of Hobbies for Stress Relief.* Verywell Mind; Verywell Mind.

https://www.verywellmind.com/the-importance-of-hobbies-for-stress-relief-3144574

Scott, E. (2019). *How social support can help you relieve stress in your life.* Verywell Mind. https://www.verywellmind.com/stress-and-social-support-research-3144460

Scott, E. (2020, June 11). *What is mindfulness?* Verywell Mind. https://www.verywellmind.com/mindfulness-the-health-and-stress-relief-benefits-3145189

Scott, E. (2024, February 12). *What is body scan meditation?* Verywell Mind. https://www.verywellmind.com/body-scan-meditation-why-and-how-3144782

Shur, M. (2021, December 15). *90 Support Quotes to Inspire You to Help Others.* Www.quoteambition.com. https://www.quoteambition.com/support-quotes/#:~:text=90%20Support%20Quotes%20to%20Inspire%20You%20to%20Help

Sizelove, V. (2023, December 21). *Internal vs. External Stressors: What's the Difference? | Find A Therapist.* Www.find-a-Therapist.com. https://www.find-a-therapist.com/internal-vs-external-stressors/

Sullivan, D. (2012, April 10). *How Stress May Trigger Smoking and How to Effectively Cope.* Healthline. https://www.healthline.com/health/heart-disease/stress-smoking#Healthy-Ways-to-Cope

Sutton, J. (2019, April 9). *What Is Mindfulness? Definition + Benefits (Incl. Psychology).* PositivePsychology.com. https://positivepsychology.com/what-is-mindfulness/

Swales, S. A. (2024, April 23). *Is Fear Running Your Life? | Psychology Today.* Www.psychologytoday.com.

https://www.psychologytoday.com/us/blog/lessons-from-a-burnt-out-psychologist/202404/is-fear-running-your-life

Telloian, C. (2021, October 4). *Mindful Breathing: Benefits, Types, and How To*. Psych Central. https://psychcentral.com/health/mindful-breathing#exercises-and-scripts

THC Editorial Team. (2021, October 14). *Present-Moment awareness: Overview, benefits, and practice*. The Human Condition. https://thehumancondition.com/present-moment-awareness/

The Knowledge Academy. (2023). *What Is Effective Communication: Key Principles and Strategies*. Www.theknowledgeacademy.com. https://www.theknowledgeacademy.com/blog/what-is-effective-communication/

Tsaousides, T. (2019). *7 Things You Need to Know About Fear*. Psychology Today. https://www.psychologytoday.com/us/blog/smashing-the-brainblocks/201511/7-things-you-need-know-about-fear

Verma, V. (2018, December 22). *The Four Types of Fear*. Foundation for Conscious Living. https://foundationforconsciousliving.org/research-and-more-wisdom/the-four-types-of-fear/

Villines, Z. (2021, October 25). *Behavioral activation: How it works, examples, and more*. Www.medicalnewstoday.com. https://www.medicalnewstoday.com/articles/behavioral-activation#how-to-try-it

Vogel, K. (2022, October 27). *The Long-Term Effects of Stress: Physical and Mental Effects*. Psych Central. https://psychcentral.com/stress/long-term-effects-of-chronic-stress-on-body-and-mind#physical-effects

Vriak, A. (2023, March 4). *Body Scan Meditation: A Complete Guide.* Mindfulness Exercises. https://mindfulnessexercises.com/meditation/body-scan/

Wade, D. (2022, July 6). *Causes of Stress: Types of Stress, Symptoms & Tips.* Psych Central. https://psychcentral.com/stress/what-causes-stress#tips

What Is Effective Communication? Skills for Work, School, and Life. (2024, May 22). Coursera. https://www.coursera.org/articles/communication-effectiveness?msockid=04ebe4c2f2246d453f6cf7cbf3076c25

Wilkinson, J. (2023, October 18). *The Joy of Hobbies: Exploring Interests and Developing Skills.* Surviving the Day. https://www.survivingtheday.com/the-joy-of-hobbies-exploring-interests-and-developing-skills/

Zinn, K. (2017, June 18). *49 Profound Mindfulness Quotes to Inspire Your Practice.* PositivePsychology.com. https://positivepsychology.com/mindfulness-quotes/#mindfulness-quotes

Printed in Great Britain
by Amazon